Power and Practices

Power and Practices
Engaging the Work of John Howard Yoder

Edited By
Jeremy M. Bergen and Anthony G. Siegrist

Foreword By
Glen Harold Stassen

 **Herald Press**
Waterloo, Ontario
Scottdale, Pennsylvania

Library and Archives Canada Cataloguing in Publication

Power and practices : engaging the work of John Howard Yoder / edited by
Jeremy M. Bergen and Anthony G. Siegrist.
 Includes bibliographical references.
 ISBN 978-0-8361-9447-0
 1. Yoder, John Howard. I. Bergen, Jeremy M., 1975- II. Siegrist, Anthony G.,
1979-
 BX8143.Y59P69 2009   230'.97092   C2008-907533-1

POWER AND PRACTICES
Copyright © 2009 by Herald Press, Scottdale, Pa. 15683
 Published simultaneously in Canada by Herald Press,
 Waterloo, Ont. N2L 6H7. All rights reserved
International Standard Book Number: 978-0-8361-9447-0
Library of Congress Catalog Card Number: 2008941354
Canadiana Entry Number: C2008-907533-1
Printed in the United States of America
Book design by Joshua Byler
Cover by Reuben Graham

14 13 12 11 10 09   10 9 8 7 6 5 4 3 2 1

To order or request information please call 1-800-245-7894
or visit www.heraldpress.com.

Contents

Foreword

Sixty-five emerging new scholars participated in the conference "Inheriting John Howard Yoder: A New Generation Examines His Thought," May 24-26, 2007, at the Toronto Mennonite Theological Centre. The breadth and depth of interest in Yoder's theological ethics by the coming generation of scholars was truly impressive. I was struck by the insightfulness of the papers that were presented, as evidenced by *Power and Practices: Engaging the Work of John Howard Yoder*.

Younger scholars, devoting their time and research at the beginning of their careers, and looking from new angles, may be able to read Yoder more carefully than some older scholars who formed their impressions two or three decades ago and have therefore not paid enough precise attention to the later prolific and posthumous writings of Yoder, which are still emerging in striking ways. These scholars *have* paid attention, and have new and important insights to offer.

Chris K. Huebner asks, "How should we receive or appropriate Yoder's thought?" By digging deeply and carefully into its profundity, I argue. Yoder has so very many strengths and dimensions of faithfulness that beginning with understanding him well can give us a depth that we will not find elsewhere. Yoder's thought is Christ-centered; it takes Christ as Lord over all of life rather than only over one "kingdom," does accurate exegesis of Jesus' way, develops the meaning of normative practices that form and shape churches' community as well as guide ethics in the world, calls us to continuous repentance and learning rather than being stuck in unfaithful ideologies, shows how to reform tradition to be faithful to Christ rather than to be servile to traditionalism, works out the implications of nonviolence, engages in incisive dialogue with theological ethics from other perspectives, and works out implications more systematically than the rest of us have done. It gives us a self-critical tradition to work in. We start far ahead of where we would be if we tried to start from scratch. But we can also "extend a Yoderian mode of theological analysis into new domains." That is what this book does.

Philip E. Stoltzfus writes: Yoder "believed himself to be an occasional thinker—self-consciously operating as a counterpoint to what one would commonly identify as systematic, or foundational, ethical and theological approaches. His critical niche involved countering, in an ad hoc way, the 'isms' and methodologies that appeared to" minimize, ignore, or distort Jesus' ethic. This gave Yoder's writing and teaching not only an occasional nature, but often a confrontational nature—as is also true of Jesus. Once I said to neuropsychologist Warren Brown that I need a blunt friend who will correct me when I get off. He replied, "we all need several blunt friends." We all need some confrontation now and then. The kingdom of God is good news, and it is also a call for repentance. Yoder does that for us.

Yoder's "occasional" nature was also "incarnational," in the sense that he *entered into* the context and questions of persons to whom he spoke and for whom he wrote. His multilingualism is a symbol of his incarnational method. He spoke German in Basel, Dutch in translating Berkhov's *Christ and the Powers*, Spanish in Argentina—and French in Alsace Lorraine and life-long at home with Annie. He entered into contexts where he was. He extended his own theological ethics by engaging with the thought of others. That is the model for how to appropriate Yoder: first enter into Yoder's own thinking, and then extend Yoder into another realm of discourse. The essays in this book follow that model.

I particularly identify with Nekeisha Alexis-Baker's way of extending Yoder's thought. Delores S. Williams says Jesus' suffering on the cross often gets used to persuade black women to submit to suffering and not rebel against injustice and then advocates removing the cross from the center of Christian proclamation. Alexis-Baker shows that Yoder makes the same criticism but then offers the right correction.

Yoder makes clear that the cross is no endorsement of passive suffering; it is the result of Jesus' actively confronting an unjust order. Therefore, it gives strength to our resistance against injustice. And at the same time the cross is Christ's compassion, identifying with outcasts and the victims of greed, domination, and violence. So those who suffer from such oppression are not alone; God in Christ suffers with them, with powerful compassion.

Alexis-Baker writes that the cross "remains essential to Jesus' story and to Black spirituality. Jesus' crucifixion is still a focal point in Black preaching and teaching, and an indispensable symbol that unifies this community in its struggle for freedom and equality. . . . Womanists challenge Christian traditions that spiritualize and make irrelevant the words and work of Christ. They also name his suffering on the cross as a result of human sin and of Jesus' confrontation with that sin, instead of seeing the cross as a divine act to be glorified." This is what Yoder insists on. The cross calls us to identify compassionately with those who suffer from injustice, and to confront the causes of the injustice.[1]

Alexis-Baker then extends her treatment one creative step farther: "Christ's call to a peculiar servanthood enables the subordinate person to be free within an unjust order, even as it calls people at the top of the social hierarchy to change their behavior and lower their position in the hierarchy. . . . Yoder contends that, far from a blind acceptance of social mores, early Christians were creatively helping those experiencing injustice to see that Christ has already liberated them and that the resurrection has already defeated the old hierarchical order."

Yoder's term, "revolutionary subordination," intends to affirm this freedom and creativity. "Viewed from a womanist perspective, revolutionary subordination has transformative potential for Black women because it advocates seizing opportunities for greater liberation." But the term is an obstacle to understanding Yoder's argument. "A more positive and understandable term like 'creative transformation'—which Yoder also uses— might be more helpful."[2] Alexis-Baker thus models probing Yoder's depth from within, and extending it in dialogue with other insights.

Similarly Andrew Brubacher Kaethler writes that "The challenge for the next generation of Anabaptist-Mennonite theological thinking is to continue to work with and develop the key insights and stances in Yoder's project." He then extends it to dialogue with scholasticism. Branson Parler puts Yoder in dialogue with Neo-Calvinists Mouw and Kuyper, seeking connection with their advocacy of the state as an order of providence or preservation. Richard Bourne suggests a way to extend Yoder's thought via Foucault and argues incisively that Yoder's understanding of commitment in community in response to God's election indicates that Oliver O'Donovan has misinterpreted him.[3] Paul C. Heidebrecht extends Yoder's theological ethics to describe how formation in churches takes place over time. Andy Alexis-Baker extends his interpretation of Yoder's understanding of pacifism into his own criticism of just policing.[4] And John C. Nugent explicitly writes on "Extending the Insights of John Howard Yoder," showing incisively and insightfully how to interpret the two testaments in relation to biblical warfare.

In his last years before his untimely death, Yoder was extending his own thinking into deepening our understanding of Jesus' roots in non-territorial Judaism, correcting Marcionite tendencies of theological ethicists who neglect those roots, and correcting sectarian and reductionistic interpretations of his own thought.

Paul Martens does internal analysis rather than extension, although I suspect extension to Stanley Hauerwas and Michael Baxter lurks in the background. Martens rightly notices that "Yoder's anti-sectarian emphasis finally reaches its zenith in these later works." Yoder intentionally moved to distinguish himself from what he saw as a sectarian approach.[5] Instead, he paid increasing attention to Jesus' and the churches' roots in Israel—and especially the prophets Jeremiah and Isaiah. But nowhere does he set the prophets or Israel or his sociological speech against theological, eschatological, or pneumatological speech. His point throughout *For the Nations* is against the either/or assumption that God and the Spirit are in one world and politics in another. "The choice or the tension which the Bible is concerned with is not between politics and something else which is not politics, but between right politics and wrong politics. Not between 'spirit' and something else which is not spiritual, but between true and false spirits. . . . Our first need has been to deny a dualism, to reject the splitting apart of territories separating the political from the nonpolitical."[6]

In my own writing, I am seeking to develop greater attention to the work of participative grace and the Holy Spirit, and transformative eschatology, as an *extension* of what Yoder pointed to, and by no means a rejection of his profound guidance, for which I am deeply and passionately grateful. I am glad to join the emerging scholars in *Power and Practices* in hopes that some day I may become an emerging theological ethicist too, as these scholars already impressively are.

Glen Harold Stassen
Fuller Theological Seminary
March 2009

Notes

1. I see this as resembling important arguments by womanist theologians Jacquelyn Grant, Karen Baker-Fletcher, M. Shawn Copeland, and Cheryl Kirk-Duggan.

2. This is one reason why I write of "transforming initiatives."

3. I also credit Yoder with doing more to avoid confusion with individualistic voluntariety by his thorough emphasis on church as community, practices of community within churches, and rootage in Isaiah, Jeremiah, and Jewish Scriptures and practices.

4. In *The War of the Lamb*, ed. Glen Stassen, Mark Thiessen Nation, and Matt Hamsher (Grand Rapids, MI: Brazos Press, 2009), Yoder extends his own understanding of pacifism into nonviolent policing by United Nations peacekeepers and other social science proposals in international relations.

5. See the footnotes in the Introduction of *For the Nations*, and Yoder, "Meaning After Babble," *Journal of Religious Ethics* 24, no. 1 (1996): 135, n23.

6. John Howard Yoder, *For the Nations: Essays Public and Evangelical* (Grand Rapids, MI: Eerdmans, 1997), 222 and 223; see also 222, 228, 233, 237.

Preface

It is tempting to prognosticate about the lasting value of John Howard Yoder's theology, to play the futurist and suggest where Yoder scholarship will go next, to try and calculate whose reading of Yoder will prove dominant in the years to come. But even the best Yoder scholars (which neither of us claims to be) are finding it hard to keep up with the new material related to this Mennonite theologian—popular articles, scholarly essays, dissertations, even new versions of Yoder's own texts. It was not long ago that interactions with Yoder's work from the likes of Douglas Harink, Richard Hays, and Peter Ochs seemed a surprising new level and type of engagement. More recently Daniel Boyarin and Romand Coles, responding to Yoder's work in the areas of Christian-Jewish schism and politics respectively, have cut loose the negative assumptions that many may have had about the broad usefulness of Yoder's thought. The work of many of the contributors in this volume also testifies to the extent to which Yoder is now known and discussed in a broader range of academic settings—beyond the field of Christian ethics, beyond traditional Mennonite circles, and beyond the associates of Stanley Hauerwas. In the opening essay of this volume, Chris K. Huebner explores these issues as he discuses what it might mean to "inherit Yoder." He suggests that inheritance and receptivity are themselves themes of Yoder's work.

In the constantly expanding arena of Yoder scholarship this collection of essays takes its place alongside projects that seek to situate Yoder's thought in conversation with partners he never interacted with directly. Those that have read Yoder are undoubtedly familiar with the ongoing conversation in his work with that of Karl Barth, Franklin Littell, the Niebuhr brothers, Just War Theory and the rest of the usual cast of characters. This volume recasts the character list to place Yoder's thought in conversations with the likes of Michel Foucault, Cecil B. DeMille, womanist theology, and even the practice of engineering.

There have previously been several volumes that have explored what Yoder said on any number of subjects and how his project holds together. We now also see a proliferation of "Yoder and ___" projects that intend to further illuminate his thinking through the contrasting light of other approaches. This volume assumes these other ways of reading and interacting with Yoder, but it seeks to do something slightly different—to extend a Yoderian mode of theological analysis into new domains. In the case of several of the essays, that means some of Yoder's fundamental insights are used reflexively to critique other facets of his own work.

The theme reflected in the title of this volume, *Power and Practices*, is broadly understood. We do not suggest that the essays collected here focus tightly on either the approach to the powers seen in the work of Walter Wink or the approach to church practices common in the work of some "post-liberal" theologians. This is the case despite the fact that both of these theological trends have links to Yoder's work. Although scholarship is clearly showing that Yoder presents useful insights in areas other than biblical pacifism—though never divorced from it—the essays in this volume are part of a ubiquitous trend of diagonal proliferation. If these essays extend Yoder's project, they do not do so in parallel directions; rather, they are at times at angles with each other, not unlike Yoder scholarship generally. They do however share in the renewed sense in contemporary theology that embodiedness and concreteness are not virtues but necessities of good theological thinking. Thus, the particular power of God manifest in Jesus Christ is practical not theoretical. In various ways, the essays assembled here are wrestling with questions of power in conversation with Yoder and with the implications such questions have for social practices within and without the church.

These essays originated as presentations at a conference, "Inheriting John Howard Yoder: A New Generation Examines His Thought" held May 24-26, 2007, and hosted by the Toronto Mennonite Theological Centre (TMTC), which is a teaching and research center of Conrad Grebel University College. In keeping with TMTC's vision of the formation of scholars for church and academy, papers were invited from "newer voices." While we did not specify exactly who qualified, it is noteworthy that the presenters were neither Yoder's peers, his primary interlocutors, nor even his students. In this sense, the essays included in this volume give some concrete indication of the kinds of interpretations that may proliferate in the future.

Chris K. Huebner's essay, adapted from a keynote address on future directions in the reception of Yoder's work, may be understood as an account of what Yoder might have made of this attempt to think about what it means to inherit his theological legacy. In light of Yoder's emphases on doxology, interruptions of grace, and the concrete Christian life, he would be relatively unconcerned with the survival of a Yoderian school of thought. Huebner proposes that Yoder's gift to those who receive it is much more a theological style, or a kind of practice, rather than as a set of claims or a canon. On this score, it seems fitting that the subsequent essays by newer theological voices do not reflect a unified perspective or a set program.

In the second chapter, Philip E. Stoltzfus argues that Yoder's theological method ought to be reevaluated in light of his substantive argument for Christian nonviolence. Stoltzfus regrets that Yoder does not adopt a self-consciously constructive methodology in relation to his uses of the term *God*. The unfortunate result of Yoder's method is an unwitting perpetuation of the very images of theological violence that he is attempting to critique christologically. Yoder would have been more consistent and ultimately helpful, Stoltzfus claims, if he would have adopted a thoroughly nonviolent approach to Christian thought and life informed by an appropriately critical and constructive stance toward theological symbolization.

Continuing the theme of theological style, Andrew Brubacher Kaethler's essay examines the inconsistency between what Yoder claimed about the need for patient and good-faith interpretation of one's dialogue partner and his actual practice of caricaturing scholasticism. While Yoder's engagement with scholasticism is an important arena for positive arguments about just war and biblical authority, his oversimplification obscures the non-Constantinian resources in these traditions. Given the centrality of reception and retrieval in postmodern theology, a nuanced appreciation and critique of Yoder provides a framework by which the power of interpreters does not dominate the interpreted.

In chapter 4, Branson Parler reassesses Yoder's engagement with a different discourse—that of the Neo-Calvinist Reformed tradition in general and its doctrine of creation in particular. Despite Yoder's critique of the *abuse* of the doctrine of creation, Parler argues that the doctrine undergirds Yoder's thinking on the Powers, their original goodness, subsequent fallenness, and ultimate redemption. The clues Yoder gives that indicate that the redemption accomplished in Jesus is not only a "new creation" (discontinuity) but also a restoration or renewal of creation (continuity) provide a key basis for dialogue between the Mennonite and Reformed traditions.

The question of power is central in the dialogue Nekeisha Alexis-Baker facilitates in chapter 5 between Yoder and various womanist theologians. Her goal is to show how Yoder's theology supports and challenges womanist critiques of the cross as a source of oppression for Black women. Nekeisha Alexis-Baker demonstrates how the cross has functioned in Black subjugation from slavery to the present and outlines various ways womanists redefine the cross in response to that oppression. She argues that Yoder's theology of the cross, particularly his naming of what the cross is not and his concept of revolutionary subordination, can aid in the womanist project of redefining the meaning of the cross for Black women's liberation.

In chapter 6, Richard Bourne presents a theology of governmental power and of Christian witness to the state. He works first with the concepts of eschatology and exile, which are both explicit in Yoder's theology. His third topic is only tacitly present—election. Bourne combines his exploration of Yoder's theology with the claim that the later work of Michel Foucault, particularly his notion of "governmentality," gives us resources for understanding what non-Constantinian forms of political critique might look like. Bourne intends to show that attentiveness to what Yoder and Foucault have to say can help the church to be a more truly ordered and political community than is the state.

How Yoder's thought supports the mandate and practical capacity of the church to be a particular kind of community is assessed in the two chapters that follow. Paul C. Heidebrecht highlights Yoder's pejorative view of engineering only to argue that Yoder himself thinks like an engineer. He shows how Yoder's interventionist perspective on church history and his non-sacramental view of church practices opens him up to the same kind of criticism he makes of efforts to take control of history. Heidebrecht then suggests that having the mind of an engineer is not ultimately problematic for the church, assuming that engineering is understood as a practice that depends upon heuristics and tacit skills more than theoretical reasoning and a desire for control.

In chapter 8, Paul Martens observes the striking diversity of those Christian and secular thinkers appropriating Yoder's ethics. He suggests that this diversity can be correlated to stages in Yoder's development. Yoder's earlier texts support an account of "eschatology as particular history" in contrast to the Social Gospel's account of "history as universal eschatology." However, Martens traces the increasing role of Jeremiah as a sign of Yoder's developing position in which history becomes a universal eschatology and church practices become instrumental. It is this last "not-particularly Christian" socio-political argument that is the point of departure for secular appropriations.

Andy Alexis-Baker contests the recent use of Yoder's writings in the development of a global theology of policing. In this ninth chapter, he argues that while Yoder deployed "policing" as a conceptual tool to critique the present, it is unwarranted to extrapolate from it a positive theory or program. From a sifting of Yoder's ad hoc comments on policing, Andy Alexis-Baker concludes that Yoder was trying to shift the debate away from whether Christians should participate in policing to a broader analysis in which the absence of violence does not necessarily denote the absence of oppression.

The question of God and power is poignantly focused by the interpretive challenges posed by warfare in the Bible. In the final chapter, John C. Nugent sketches Yoder's unique contribution to this discussion and revises Yoder's narration in order to overcome important deficiencies. The heart of Yoder's argument is that Israel should never have constituted itself as a centralized monarchial nation with a standing army and that the exile was God's way of correcting this misstep and preparing his people for nonviolent witness and global mission. The "problem" of Old Testament warfare is the reader's failure to discern, in Scripture, how from the very beginning God identified bloodshed as a problem and has been shaping his people ever since to resist its deadly allure.

In addition to the essential role of the Toronto Mennonite Theological Centre and Conrad Grebel University College, several other institutions must be commended for their support of the original conference: Wycliffe College, Eastern Mennonite Seminary, and Associated Mennonite Biblical Seminary. The support of Herald Press began with the conference and has multiplied through the process of publication. Likewise, we thank all those who participated in the conference, neophytes and senior scholars alike, whose presence and engagement helped sharpen the contents of this volume.

What was dubbed "the Yoder project"—first a series of seminars throughout the year, then a conference, and now a book—was the vision and initiative of Jonathan Seiling, the convener of the TMTC Fellows Group, who worked with us as the organizing committee. We are both very grateful for the collegiality and friendship of the members of the TMTC Fellows Group, which in 2007 consisted of about fifteen Mennonites and fellow travelers in doctoral programs at the Toronto School of the Theology. This community has been an important place for us to engage in collaborative and interdisciplinary theological thinking, in a way that reminded all of us to consider the implications of our academic work for the lives of our faith communities. It is our hope that this set of engagements with Yoder's work will be received in this spirit.

Jeremy M. Bergen
Anthony G. Siegrist

Chapter 1

The Work of Inheritance:
Reflections on Receiving John Howard Yoder

Chris K. Huebner

In 1952, four years after his graduation from Goshen College, John Howard Yoder wrote a letter to Harold S. Bender, his former teacher and then patriarch of North American Anabaptist-Mennonite studies. Reflecting on his attempt to come to grips with what he had learned from Bender, Yoder explained: "What has happened to me is that in the process of growing up, I have put together an interest in Anabaptism, which you gave me, an MCC [Mennonite Central Committee] experience to which you were instrumental in assigning me, and theological study to which you directed me, to come out with what is a more logical fruition of your own convictions than you yourself realize."[1]

Thirty-six years later, speaking as president of the Society of Christian Ethics, Yoder articulated an account of what he called "seeing history doxologically." "To see history doxologically," he claimed, "is to be empowered and obligated to discern, down through the centuries, which historical developments can be welcomed as progress in the light of the Rule of the Lamb and which as setbacks."[2] He suggests, further, that "[a] doxological commitment should free us from the self-contradictory but still widely practiced worldliness of those who, when the trends go against their tastes, decry them, yet when the trends go 'the right way' claim them as validation."[3] The doxological task of the Christian is, then, "to own the Lamb's victory in one's own time."[4] And yet it needs to be added that this doxological conception of receiving a history is shot through with

radically transformative images of messianic rupture: "To see history doxologically demands and enables that we appropriate especially/specifically
those modes of witness which explode the limits of our capacity to be illu-
minated and led."[5]

I offer these two sets of comments as bookends that encapsulate
Yoder's theological career and in doing so draw attention to an important theme that runs throughout his work as a whole. The first no doubt
reflects a spirit of youthful enthusiasm and confidence but also a sense of
compulsion and responsibility that foregrounds a theological project not
yet formally begun. While some may be tempted to hear in these words
a dismissive hint of arrogance, perhaps even ungratefulness, I think they
display rather an awareness of having been given an extraordinary gift
and a recognition that it remains necessary to make sense of what it
means to receive such an inheritance.

The second set of comments may come dressed up in the more
refined tones of an established scholar. And yet they equally reflect a concern with the questions of inheritance and receptivity, albeit one that is
more broadly construed as a specifically theological inheritance and an
ethos of Christian receptivity more generally. Indeed, I want to suggest
that this appreciation of the need to struggle through the difficult task of
receiving an inheritance, the arduous labor of memory, the complex set
of negotiations, arguments, and interpretations involved in embodying a
tradition weaves its way throughout Yoder's entire body of work in various ways.

More specifically, by highlighting these themes, I want to emphasize
the significance of Yoder's appreciation of what we might call the work of
inheritance. Throughout his meandering engagements and conversations,
we constantly find Yoder striving to articulate a posture with respect to
history that does not reflect a possessive will to somehow manage and
control it. Or to echo Yoder's own words, he is interested in exploring
how we might receive the simultaneously gracious and dangerous memory
of Christ's cross and resurrection in a manner that does not give in to the
temptation to outfit history with "handles," to lay hold to it, and thus
attempt to "move it in the right direction."[6]

At times he speaks of this in terms of faithfulness, at other times in
terms of witness, and still at other times in terms of peoplehood. In certain
places, his preferred rhetorical style is essentially critical, as in his interpretations of Constantinianism, or his objections to an ethos of triumphal or

establishmentarianism more generally. At other places he paints a more constructive picture of the stance of radical reformation, of diasporic scattering, or the practice of hermeneutic patience. To make too much of any one of these descriptions would be to embark on a search for a conceptual anchor of a system that does not, as such, exist.

None of these favorite tropes is put forward as an attempt to provide a new or better handle of some sort. Rather, they offer us glimpses of a way of life whose identity might be said to consist precisely in its not coinciding with itself, in its ongoing performance of receptivity. They provide a vision of a body whose being is not premised on the presumed goodness of its own continued survival but embodies a stance of dispossession.

What is most important for the purposes of this discussion is to see that in each of these moments we find Yoder wrestling with the questions of inheritance and receptivity. His work is everywhere laced with notions of memory and hope, of historical discernment and openness to the surprises of the new. But these themes are not to be understood in a manner that suggests a simple and straightforward activity of repetition, of narrowly factual accuracy, or of what we might describe as archival sensibilities. Neither do they present a vision of hope that consists in the desire to realize some given end, as if the future somehow rests squarely on our shoulders. They reflect neither a primitivist or preservationist reification of the past, nor a progressivist construal of hope as a future goal to be achieved. Rather, we find in Yoder a vision of inheritance that is interruptive and radically transforms those who are in a position to receive it. Indeed, echoing Barth, he emphasizes that it is not so much we who remember, but rather that we are made a part of God's memory, and in being so remembered have our very we-ness redefined. At the very least, the question of receiving an inheritance is, for Yoder, far from straightforward. Inheritance names a kind of work, a life's work of ongoing transformation in which the very identity of the one said to be doing the receiving is somehow part of what's at stake.

In all this, I can't help but hear in Yoder's work echoes of some attempts to describe religious life by those who have been influenced by Wittgenstein. Raimond Gaita, for example, summarizes the grammar of Christianity as follows: "one [does] not first believe in God and then as a further step, perhaps of inference or perhaps of faith, believe that the world as He created it is a good world. Belief in God as the creator of heaven and earth is inseparable from gratitude for the world."[7] Or as

Fergus Kerr puts it, "It is because people exult and lament, sing for joy, bewail their sins and so on that they are able, eventually, to have thoughts about God. Worship is not the result but the precondition of believing in God."[8] Translated into the present context, it might be suggested that we do not first inherit beliefs and then ask what to make of them. Inheritance is not a first step, which admits of later hermeneutic clarifications. Rather, Christian belief, according to Yoder, is essentially the work of inheritance. The Christian life is inseparable from a struggle with the ongoing practice of receptivity.

In an attempt to identify some of the more specific aspects of what this work of inheritance involves, I want to highlight what I take to be one of the richer and more illuminating discussions of Yoder to appear in recent years, that of the political theorist Romand Coles. Through a series of insightful and informative readings of a range of key texts, Coles demonstrates Yoder's commitment to what he calls a political hermeneutics of vulnerable receptivity or receptive generosity. In particular, he argues that Yoder's theology crucially involves a vision of tradition as an ongoing dialogical process that requires careful attention to outsiders and a healthy awareness of its own fallibility. As Coles himself puts it, Yoder's understanding of Christianity as radical reformation

> calls for multiple particular vulnerable encounters in which the strengths of the church body are little by little brought to light and perhaps themselves radically reformed and renewed. . . . The heralding, discernment, risk, and renewal of faithfulness occur to a great extent in the contestatory and cooperative work around particular historically situated questions.[9]

Echoing Deleuze's contrast between rhizomatic and arboreal imaginations, Coles helpfully draws attention to Yoder's claim that tradition is best understood not as a tree but a vine that requires constant attention, involves inevitable interruption, and an openness to growing in new directions. In particular, he underscores the significance of the following quote from Yoder: "Far from being an ongoing growth like a tree (or a family tree) the wholesome growth of a tradition is like a vine: a story of constant interruption of organic growth in favor of pruning and a new chance for roots."[10] Among other things, such a conception of receiving a tradition requires the cultivation of a readiness for ongoing reformation, renewal, and the difficult capacity to confess its failure when necessary.

The work of inheriting a tradition is thus crucially not uni-directional. It does not consist in linear gaze backward upon the past, nor does it give rise to a clear and unambiguous path looking forward. Rather, it involves a constant "looping back" to the origins in light of unpredictable, often surprising encounters with other dialogue partners. As Coles himself puts it, it is simultaneously teleological and ateleological. While its movement is disciplined rather than random, it is not merely theoretically open to surprises and unexpected moments of grace but actively attentive to them.

The traditioned work of inheritance is, in other words, not first of all a project of retrieval that operates out of an archivists desire for preservation. Rather, its engagement with the past is necessarily generative of new conversations and dialogue partners. By way of identifying one such dialogue partner with whom I think it would be valuable to bring Yoder into more explicit conversation, let me suggest that such a reading of tradition, inheritance, and receptivity is strikingly similar to Rowan Williams' claim that the inheritance of Scripture and tradition involves a practice of what he calls "making difficult." Williams writes,

> Scripture and tradition require to be read in a way that brings out their strangeness, their non-obvious and non contemporary qualities, in order that they may be read both freshly and truthfully from one generation to another. They need to be made more *difficult* before we can accurately grasp their simplicities. Otherwise, we read with eyes not our own and think them through with minds not our own; the "deposit of faith" does not really come into contact with *ourselves*. And this "making difficult," this confession that what the gospel says in Scripture and tradition does not instantly and effortlessly make sense, is perhaps one of the most fundamental tasks for theology.[11]

In short, for Williams as for Yoder, to inherit a tradition is not a straightforward process of repetition but a complex exercise of receptivity that will no doubt encounter numerous surprises, ruptures, and difficulties.

As we now find ourselves two or three generations after Yoder's most well-known work and more than a decade after his death, it is not surprising that a younger generation of scholars finds itself inclined to reflect on what it means to go about inheriting and receiving the theological legacy he has left us. Indeed, in light of Yoder's dismissals of trend watching, his suspicion of a generational, family-tree understanding of tradition, not to mention his hermeneutics of messianic interruption, I think it is only right if we tremble a bit in asking what it might mean to inherit John Howard Yoder. Just as interpretations of Wittgenstein's rejection of the urge to produce theses and theories in philosophy so easily lapse into the articulation of new theses and theories, so readings of Yoder often seem prone to adopt styles and stances he sought to warn us against.

Given Yoder's dialogical and ad hoc approach to doing theology, it might even be suggested that the more a reading of Yoder strives to be faithful in a literal way to repeating and capturing his main claims, the more we ought to approach it with caution. And yet I want to suggest that his claims about tradition as "looping back" and his understanding of inheritance as an ongoing task of receptivity are nevertheless useful as a way of guiding how we approach Yoder's own legacy. More specifically, I think that Yoder's own concern with the ongoing work of inheritance is something that those who have come to his work more recently would do well to pay special attention to. But if it is appropriate to suggest that the work of inheritance is so central to Yoder's own work, as I have been arguing, it is equally important to understand that it appears not merely, or even primarily, as a topic about which he wrote and theorized. Rather, it is a practice he sought to engage in. I have suggested elsewhere that just as important as it is to understand and examine what Yoder said, what specific claims he made and defended, it is equally important to appreciate what we might call his theological style.[12]

Here, I want to suggest that how he performs the question of inheritance is a key aspect of this style. What matters, if we are to take all of this seriously, is that the question of receiving Yoder is a grappling, a difficult work of contestation. And it should be emphasized that the question of what it means to inherit Yoder must somehow remain essentially open. It is certainly not something we should expect to be settled conclusively in a new collection of essays.

Where do we go from here? Among those new voices in conversation with Yoder's work, do we find a Yoder that is different in some identifiable respect? And if so, how might this difference best be characterized? To mention just a few examples, I notice that questions of church and sect are notably absent from recent engagements with Yoder's work. There is refreshingly little reference to Walter Rauschenbush and Reinhold Niebuhr and the agenda they set for an earlier generation of debates about Christian pacifism. Similarly, it might be suggested that recent discussions of Yoder are less apt to force him into the categories of hero or villain and more likely to treat him as a dialogue partner with whom it is possible to be simultaneously for and against. In other words, Yoder is approached not so much as someone to be defended or defeated as he is used and appropriated more ambiguously, but nevertheless constructively. Here one might identify Romand Coles and Daniel Boyarin.[13] This might be less true in more specifically Mennonite discussions, but I get the sense that it is starting to change there as well.

Echoing some of Yoder's own themes of inheritance discussed above, we might further ask what are some of the moments of strangeness that characterize these new discussions of Yoder? What are some of the key surprises that animate the new generation's work? To which specific moments, which texts, do we find ourselves looping back? And when we do so, through which outsiders and new developments are we approaching them anew? As far as outsiders go, I have already alluded to Wittgenstein and Deleuze. One could also mention Derrida, Foucault, Said, Virilio, Taubes, Boyarin, MacIntyre, Davidson, and Lakatos as voices who have recently been brought into conversation with Yoder. And, by association, we might also mention Wolin, Benjamin, and Agamben, among others.

There are also some more specifically theological dialogue partners to note: in addition to Williams, we notice Yoder being discussed alongside Milbank, O'Donovan, Barth, Bonhoeffer, and various womanist and liberationist voices. And there is also interest in bringing Yoder into more explicit and more constructive conversation with historical voices such as Augustine, Aquinas, and the Cappadocians, in ways that are more fruitful than some of Yoder's own encounters with those same figures.

As far as new political developments go, it is worth asking whether and, if so, how accounts of the shift from nation-state to globalization or the increasing attention being given to biopolitical models of sovereignty work their way into new discussions of Yoder's work. With respect to any new developments that emerge out of these circumstances, we must further ask which of them can be regarded as progress and which as setbacks. Is this merely another instance of trend watching? Or is there something of genuine value that is emerging out of these sorts of encounters?

By way of conclusion, I want to offer a suggestion about why Yoder's work might seem to endure. I can't help but think that the seemingly ongoing relevance of Yoder's work across multiple generations has something to do with the ad hoc, particular, nomadic, and fragmentary character of his theology. Might it be because of the simultaneous timeliness and untimeliness of his work that those in other eras hear it speaking to them? Those who write in a timeless manner in the hopes of speaking across generations are almost surely doomed to failure. So perhaps it is precisely because he did not set out to speak to us, the representatives of a so-called new generation, that Yoder seems to speak to us so richly. Then again, perhaps not.

I am fully aware that I have raised more questions than I have attempted to answer in these reflections on what it might mean to receive Yoder. And I do not presume that the questions I have identified are necessarily the most fruitful. There no doubt remain other important questions that have not yet been asked or at least taken with sufficient seriousness. But more important than striving to identify a list of questions to be asked and answered, I hope we have learned from Yoder the wisdom of adopting a style of questioning that compels us to take our inheritance seriously while freeing us from the temptation to turn it into an idol to be preserved as a matter of course.

There is no good reason to receive the work of Yoder simply for its own sake. But if a new generation is able to identify, through an engagement with Yoder, new modes of faithfulness and new examples of the truth of Christ, then that is cause for celebration. If, however, a new generation feels compelled to inherit Yoder only because that is all that an earlier generation has left them, then we stand little hope of receiving any gifts he might have to give us.

Notes

1. Quoted in Albert N. Keim, *Harold S. Bender, 1897-1962* (Scottdale, PA: Herald Press, 1998), 456.

2. John Howard Yoder, "To Serve Our God and to Rule the World," in *The Royal Priesthood: Essays Ecclesiological and Ecumenical*, ed. Michael G. Cartwright (Grand Rapids, MI: Eerdmans, 1994), 132.

3. Ibid., 139.

4. Ibid., 137.

5. Ibid., 129.

6. See John Howard Yoder, *The Politics of Jesus*, 2nd ed. (Grand Rapids, MI: Eerdmans, 1994), 228-29.

7. Raimond Gaita, *The Philosopher's Dog* (London: Routledge, 2002), 136.

8. Fergus Kerr, *Theology After Wittgenstein* (London: Blackwell, 1986), 183.

9. Romand Coles, *Beyond Gated Politics: Reflections for the Possibility of Democracy* (Minneapolis: University of Minnesota Press, 2005), 127.

10. John Howard Yoder, *The Priestly Kingdom: Social Ethics as Gospel* (Notre Dame: University of Notre Dame Press, 1984), 69, as quoted in Coles, *Beyond Gated Politics*, 115.

11. Rowan Williams, *Arius: Heresy and Tradition*, 2nd ed. (Grand Rapids, MI: Eerdmans, 2002), 236.

12. See Chris K. Huebner, *A Precarious Peace: Yoderian Explorations on Theology, Knowledge, and Identity* (Scottdale, PA: Herald Press, 2006), 22-23; 97-113.

13. See Daniel Boyarin, "Judaism as a Free Church: Footnotes to John Howard Yoder's *The Jewish-Christian Schism Revisited*," *CrossCurrents* 56, no. 4 (2007): 6-21.

Chapter 2

Nonviolent Jesus, Violent God?
A Critique of John Howard Yoder's Approach to Theological Construction

Philip E. Stoltzfus

The function of theology is to be suspicious of theology.
        —John Howard Yoder, in *Preface to Theology*

In 1956, American moviegoers were thrilled by the spectacle of steely-eyed Charlton Heston posed iconically on a rock above the Red Sea intoning the following lines with a fantastically archaic sense of self-righteousness:

> Fear not, stand still, and see the salvation of the Lord. . . .
> The Lord of Hosts will do battle for us.
> Behold His mighty hand![1]

Sixteen years later, a Mennonite from Indiana invoked these very lines as Old Testament theological grounding for his pacifist interpretation of the social ethics of Jesus:

> YHWH [is] the God who saves his people without their need-
> ing to act. . . .
> "Fear not, stand firm,
> And see the salvation of the Lord. . . .
> The Lord will fight for you,
> And you have only to be still." (Exod 14:13-14)

Every portion of the Exodus account, difficult to interpret at other points, is clear in the report that the Israelites did nothing to bring about the destruction of the Egyptians. The only call to them was to believe and obey. When they did so, the seemingly inevitable menace hanging over them disappeared.[2]

Perhaps one should draw from this unusual juxtaposition merely a lesson on the wondrously multifaceted character of the biblical tradition—that a blockbuster of American cinema and a countercultural Mennonite thinker could both claim to find such profound value in the same timeless narrative of God's defeat of the Egyptian army. And yet, what an uncomfortable theological irony this represents. Could it be that John Howard Yoder is working out of an image of God that stands in some sort of uneasy continuity with that of Cecil B. DeMille's? Could it be that, after the impressive scholarly and interpretive apparatus advocating for the plausibility of the nonviolent politics of Jesus has run its course, there remains for Yoder, at the end of the day, a horrifically violent, Hollywoodesque image of God lurking in the shadows?

Such is the thesis of Ray Gingerich, who in a 2003 *Mennonite Quarterly Review* article argues that Yoder has left us with "the biblical and theological problem of a nonviolent messiahship resting on the foundation of a violent God"—a "'sacralized Warrior-God.'"[3] In attempting to think theologically about the meaning of biblical passages having to do with the wrath, vengeance, and "wars of Yahweh," Gingerich finds that Yoder operates out of a model of "God" thoroughly compromised by the mythologies of divine and human redemptive violence. Such a stance represents an intolerable situation for Gingerich, both theologically and practically. Theologically, it introduces an anomaly into our understanding of Jesus as fully reflective of the character of God. Practically, given the reality of our twenty-first-century social setting of empire, it calls into question the coherence and viability of the church's calling to faithfully witness to its heritage of "the possibility of a nonviolent society with alternative structures."[4] Why was Yoder unable to move critically beyond the "nonviolent Jesus/violent God" paradigm? Gingerich suggests three possible causes: 1) Yoder's desire to maintain loyalty to Mennonite Church discourses and expectations, 2) his abiding commitment to Barthian biblical realism, and 3) his tendency to sacralize the ancient Hebrew worldview.[5]

Upon further exploration of this apparent problem in Yoderian thought, I want to argue that our critique should run deeper than merely adjusting our intra-Mennonite politics, our biblical hermeneutic, or our appropriation of ancient mythologies of violence. A more radical assessment of Yoder's very approach to theological method is in order. In *Preface to Theology*, for example, the early Yoder avoids developing an explicit sense of what his concept of God looks like. To be sure, he admirably traces certain (especially christological) themes in a biblically and historically developmental way, interpreting and critiquing them in light of the nonviolent Jesus. But in relation to a concept of God, Yoder does not, either in this or in later writings, even appear *interested* in entering into the discipline of theological construction. That is, he does not allow himself, to use the language of Gordon Kaufman, to reflect in a self-consciously critical and constructive manner about his uses of the term God. The result of such an evasion of theology is that it leaves us open, by implication, to the replication of pre-critical images of a domineering, violent God that the artifacts of popular culture, such as *The Ten Commandments*, loan to us by default.

I want to propose, then, three further lines of exploration that more directly challenge Yoder's conception of theological work in the context of his own cultural milieu: (1) Yoder's questionable appropriation of "Yahweh's wars" in light of Cecil B. DeMille; (2) Yoder's reticence in working imaginatively with theological metaphor; and (3) Yoder's unpersuasive critique of theological constructivism. Along the way, as a Mennonite thinker, I want to be honest and forthright about both the successes and failures that I perceive in the theological dimensions of Yoder's project.

Yoderian "Wars of Yahweh" and Cecil B. DeMille

If there is one phrase that could serve as a leitmotif for Yoder's perspective on holy war, Gingerich argues, it would be, "Yahweh is the God who saves his people without their needing to act."[6] The narrative of the rout of the Egyptian army at the Red Sea becomes in *Politics of Jesus* the foundational narrative for exilic and post-exilic Israelites as they transform the "stand still" tradition into the consciousness of a new form of nonmilitary minority political survival. Yet as Jack Nelson-Pallmeyer argues, the Exodus narrative itself is shot through with strikingly violent theological elements. Perpetrated through the ten plagues and the battle at the Red Sea, God's superior violence against large sectors of the Egyptian population, both young and old, guilty and innocent, slave and free, serves in the narrative as a supposedly necessary means for guaranteeing justice, inspiring belief, and annihilating ene-mies. In many ways, Nelson-Pallmeyer concludes, the Exodus narrative is not as liberative as we like to think, containing theological inconsis-tencies that remain disjunctive in relation to key insights of Jesus con-cerning the loving, compassionate, and nonviolent character of God.[7]

How, then, did a Mennonite thinker formed by the cultural milieu of the 1950s and 60s come to see Exodus 14:13-14 and other parallel passages in which the Israelites are told to "stand still" and watch God kill as central to a nonviolent ethic? Whether or not Yoder ever viewed the film *The Ten Commandments*, DeMille's epic had become the single most popular and influential interpretation of the Exodus narrative for the culture out of which Yoder worked, and it remains so to this day. Far from being the expression of a pacifist, suffering, believers church, Heston's "stand still" performance, by the time of *Politics of Jesus*, had been enshrined in the public consciousness as the quintessential expres-sion of God's saving acts on behalf of a Cold War nation attempting militarily to counter (as DeMille himself states in the opening mono-logue) "the whims of a dictator."[8]

To be sure, DeMille goes to considerable lengths in the screenplay to revise the biblical storyline in order to protect the justice, and even, at times, the "nonviolence" of God's character. For example, in the scene directly following the burning bush episode, Heston, ironically clutching his staff like a rifle, declares to Joshua, "It is not by the sword that He will deliver his people, but by the staff of a shepherd."[9] Furthermore, during the plagues, Pharaoh's "heart is hardened" not by God, as stated throughout chapters 7–14 of Exodus, but by Nefretiri. Also in the film, the command to send the angel of death to slaughter the firstborn comes out of the mouth of Rameses, not God as Exodus 11:4-5 states. So in certain respects, the Exodus God of American popular culture as depicted in *The Ten Commandments* is more theologically refined in relation to the issue of violence than is Yoder's handling of the God-concept in the same storyline. Yet of course, DeMille's God ends up massacring the Egyptians, as well as the idolatrous Israelites during the golden calf episode, with a special effects extravaganza of grisly wrathfulness that audiences would not soon forget. In Yoder's text, God acts to conveniently "disappear" the Egyptians. But the result is the same, and it is precisely the violent underbelly of 1950s American civil-religion "theologizing" with which Yoder's use of the Exodus story stands in uneasy continuity.

In Gingerich's reading, Yoder never intended to give the impression of advocating for a violent concept of God, and he denied to God the function of acting directly as an agent of violence or evil of any sort. Nevertheless, Yoder repeatedly pictures God as "harnessing," "channeling," and "delegating" the violence of worldly powers for purportedly positive ends.[10] Theologically, the implication we are left with is the image of a God who, through delegating violent acts, still determines "who gets destroyed and who is saved through the instrumentality of this violence."[11] Furthermore, Yoder finds an explicit, theologically constructive role for violence in the model of ancient Israelite holy war. Whether interpreted as taking place through divine or human agency, or carried out through nonmilitary means, nature miracle, or genocidal slaughter, the conquest narratives present us with the archetypal paradigm of "obedience" to Yahweh alone over against reliance on standing militia, skill in warfare, or ideologies of earthly kingship. This theological approach, in Yoder's view, opens up for first-century followers of Jesus the possibility of conceiving of the victory of God through nonviolent action, thus prompting Yoder to assert in a footnote the peculiar claim that "Hebrew holy war is the historical foundation" of "Jesus' nonviolence."[12] But would Yoder have *had* to make such a theological move, such a pledge of allegiance, at least indirectly, to the image of the warrior-God of the conquest?

I think that Gingerich perhaps goes too far in his critique of Yoder, in particular on the point of Yoder's attempt to make constructive use of Old Testament materials. Yoder's acknowledgment of the language of vengeance, wrath, and warfare in certain biblical texts indicates, it seems to me, more the presence of a rhetorical device to de-center the ethical dualisms of his interlocutors than it does considered judgment, in some sort of deliberative or normative way, concerning the character of God. Indeed, as Gingerich himself argues, the Barthian understanding of vengeance and wrath that informs Yoder's usages could be re-interpreted as pointing more toward the state of human fallibility than toward direct description of divine character. Furthermore, I think the biblical text itself could have provided Yoder more adequate resources for developing a non-violence hermeneutic than the "stand still" and related "obedience" themes would suggest—the biblical sources by no means give "unqualified endorsement of holy war as 'obedience' to YHWH."[13] Parallel to his identification in *Preface to Theology* of three parallel theologies in the New Testament—Paul, John, and the writer of Hebrews[14]—Yoder could have characterized the Hebrew texts as representing a conversation among competing models of God. That is, he could have more adequately acknowledged the ways in which the warrior-God tradition becomes significantly relativized through the prophetic, priestly, wisdom, and apocalyptic strands of tradition.

In Genesis 18:22-33 and Exodus 32:1-14, for example, we find options for radically questioning the role of violence in the character of God. Abraham and Moses both challenge God to scale back his threat to annihilate, respectively, the city of Sodom and the Israelite worshippers of the golden calf. In addition to obedience and patience, we find models in the patriarchs of *dis*obedience and *im*patience in the face of certain seemingly unjust, or arbitrarily violent, conceptions of God's intention and character. As it is, Yoder's appropriation of the "stand still" theme remains theologically suspect, especially in the face of an image of God who is in the process of, at least in certain texts in Joshua as well as in the later scenes of *The Ten Commandments*, committing mass murder. Does Yoder advocate for theology to "Stand still and allow God to commit genocide?" Abraham and Moses don't stand for it. They protest, they raise their voice. They challenge the very image of such a God. They get in the way. By contrast, Yoder remains, theologically, silent.

Yoder and Theological Imagination

One of the ironies of labeling Yoder a theologian—as opposed to social ethicist, historian, biblical scholar, or even philosopher[15]—is that he behaves in a curiously evasive manner when it comes to giving attention to the image of the One on whom the theological discipline typically focuses: God. To be sure, language about God is ever present in his thinking; however, almost never does the concept, symbol, or image of God itself—that very name that he himself invokes and the imaginative resources he brings to bear in making that invocation—come under his own critical scrutiny. For a thinker like Gordon Kaufman, the clarification of where one stands in relation to the regulative conceptual elements of the Christian worldview—God, Christ, human, world—is a healthy and necessary exercise in epistemological humility in the face of one's subject matter.[16] In other words, our concept of God is always already bound up with, informed by, or (as the case may be) contaminated by our understandings of who we think Jesus is, and who we think we are as human agents within the hermeneutical environment. Why is it that Mennonite theology in the Yoderian tradition will spend decades trying to get its biblical hermeneutic, christology, ecclesiology, and historiography worked out exactly right, but hand the image of God over to everybody else (i.e., the non-pacifist majority) to define, articulate, and poeticize about for us or on our behalf? Is it any wonder that, after refusing to do theology, we subsequently discover that the picture of God that has been handed back to us in our popular culture and that we find ourselves intoning by default as a part of the music of our language—then needing to do linguistic and mental back flips in order to legitimate and defend—turns out to be a disturbingly violent one?

Gingerich, in a recent unpublished article, identifies in a crystalline way the structure of this problem for Mennonite theology. The model before us of a warrior-God coupled with a nonviolent, Jesus-informed social ethic, Gingerich writes, leads to an untenable theological and ethical dilemma:

> Ascribing a necessary behavior and way-of-being to God that is forbidden by God for the followers of Jesus is a peculiarly fateful flaw in pacifist and Anabaptist theologies. For if God is violent, and God—however we may conceive of God—is Power, then power in the final analysis is violence. And if violence is a characteristic of God, and we hold that Jesus is the fullest revelation of God available to us, then we cannot, in truth, believe that Jesus is nonviolent. And if Jesus is not nonviolent, then we who claim that as Christians our lives must be in conformity with the teachings and example of Jesus are in error.[17]

The influence between understandings of God, Christ, and Christian discipleship that Gingerich lays out so logically here does not necessarily express itself in a straight, determinately causative line. Dysfunctional images of God and Christ can distort our practice, and alternatively, dysfunctional practice can distort our images. Failure to acknowledge and address the fissures and tensions within these bewildering cycles of symbol and practice, particularly in relation to the concept of God, can lead to all sorts of psychological, pastoral, and ecclesiological unintended consequences, as Nelson-Pallmeyer argues: "[I]t is difficult to hold together a nonviolent Jesus with a violent God. Doing so allows us to project our own unresolved violence onto God, internalize it, and repress hatred of people and institutions with whom we disagree."[18]

What is helpful in the case of Yoder is to bring to the table a more adequate engagement with the creative and imaginative dimensions of the theological enterprise. Drawing upon the thinkers in the constructivist tradition like Kaufman and Sallie McFague, I would argue, can help us clarify the way forward when we sense the need to critique metaphorical constructs of God. The first thing to affirm, from Kaufman's perspective, is the *aseity* of God—that to which our metaphors and constructs point remains ultimately "mystery," beyond our ability to control or manipulate. Or to use the language of Yoder, "Providence remains inscrutable."[19] Furthermore, our constructs themselves are never simple descriptions or correspondences to theological states-of-affairs but are always already shrouded in Barthian fallenness, tainted by the Feuerbacherian projections of our own wants and desires. Thus we are responsible, say Kaufman and McFague, for the images we choose to select and propagate. Attempting to pass off onto Scripture and tradition responsibility for the language we favor can be a mark of theological laziness or even maliciousness. The formulation of Yoder himself from *Preface to Theology* is apropos, here: "'theology' is the label for that realm of human endeavor where people are careful and accountable about the language they use about God."[20]

In taking up our accountability for given proposals for language about God, we are counseled by McFague to think of the metaphors and analogies as "heuristic" devices—thought experiments that must be tested and refined through conversation and experience.[21] Far from being an intellectualistic or rationalistic enterprise, McFague's method, drawing upon feminist and ecological resources, involves investigation of the concrete, feeling-endowed, motivational, and embodied character of the metaphorical materials under consideration. Thus she can juxtapose the traditional "monarchical" model of God with the equally traditional, if much less attested model of "the world as God's body," comparing and contrasting the two, testing their limits and inadequacies, weighing their appropriateness for speaking to the pastoral and political concerns of the day, yet never relinquishing the monotheistic backdrop that pervades the whole investigation.[22]

Yoder himself, in his late article "Thinking Theologically from a Free-Church Perspective," demonstrates a process of metaphorical critique strikingly similar to moves in both McFague and Kaufman:

All communication about God must use analogies from the human world. Yet every analogy has limits. That "Yahweh is King" is the central Hebrew doxology; that "Jesus Christ is Lord" is its Christian counterpart. Jesus taught his followers to call God "Father." Yet there are meanings of "King," "Lord," and "Father" that are inappropriate, because they connote oppression. The perspective of the cross, of the victim, of the outsider, of the slave or the child or the woman is a necessary corrective to wrong uses of analogy, especially to such usages as might support power gradients instead of undoing them as the Gospel does.[23]

Here is an example of Yoder engaging his theological mind. He interrogates the analogies or images used to assert central claims about the character of God, both Old Testament "King," and New Testament "Lord and Father," and finds that, in certain conversations, under certain conditions, they should not be used.

But what is missing here? Yoder does not mention in this brief paragraph the most problematic image of all from a nonviolence perspective, the symbol of God as warrior, arising out of the so-called "wars of Yahweh" tradition. Doesn't the construct of the warrior-God who delegates, channels, or orders vengeance and wrath upon human beings connote precisely the oppressive situation about which Yoder is concerned? Is not the assertion of the violence of God, be it in holy war, atonement theory, or apocalyptic cataclysm, precisely that which (to use Yoder's language) acts to "support" the very "power gradients" that must be undone "as the Gospel does"?

I believe the necessary corrective here is to propose a stance of preaching, praying, living, thinking, and acting out of an image of God constructed from thoroughly nonviolent symbolic materials, as a matter of programmatic conviction, based upon one's location in the present believing community. Some interpreters want to project just such a reconstructed God image into Yoder's work. Nancey Murphy, for example, finds the "hard core" of Yoder's theology to be "the moral character of God [as] revealed in Jesus' vulnerable enemy love and renunciation of domination."[24] Similarly, Harry Huebner finds the Yoderian perspective on the biblical storyline as showing "God to be the ultimate moral force, because within God's being lies the ground of moral truth."[25] But neither Murphy nor Huebner offer in their articles a single example of Yoder explicitly using the language of the "moral character" or "moral force" of God, or indeed of Yoder constructively investigating "God's being" in any way whatsoever. Yoder rarely makes theological moves of that sort in his writing. He neither explicitly takes up the problem of violence in the image of God nor does he explicitly propose an alternative. More recent writers, such as Nelson-Pallmeyer, J. Denny Weaver, Ted Grimsrud, and Ray Gingerich, *do* unequivocally make these steps in relation to an image of divine nonviolence. Gingerich, for example, calls for "perceiving (constructing) a new reality of power—power as the Nonviolence-of-God."[26]

Yoder gives us some hints along the way, however. In *The Original Revolution* he refers to "the undiscriminating and unconditional character of [God's] love."[27] In *Politics of Jesus* he states that "Obedience means . . . reflecting the character of the love of God."[28] And in the very last sentence of his 1980 introduction to *Yahweh Is a Warrior*, he invokes "Yahweh's shalom-bringing power."[29] Is this the image of God upon which Yoder is going to stand? Or is it rather the image where God is delegating and channeling violence? The reader cannot tell. But the reader *should* be able to tell.

Yoder and Theological Construction

Thus in reflecting on Yoder's materials while working with concepts of God in this way, we face a more fundamental difficulty having to do with the conception of theological work itself that we find in Yoder. As many of his interpreters have noted, he engaged throughout his life in a genre of writing best described as "occasional." Furthermore, he believed himself to be an occasional thinker—self-consciously operating as a counterpoint to what one would commonly identify as systematic, or foundational, ethical and theological approaches.[30] His critical niche involved countering, in an ad hoc way, the "isms" and methodologies that appeared to him to relativize the social ethic of Jesus. The disadvantage of this dialogical stance is best illustrated, I believe, through comparison with the approach of Kaufman. In *God the Problem, An Essay on Theological Method* and later books, Kaufman articulates a view of theology as "imaginative construction," a position that characterizes, in his view, both (1) the dimension of human imagination and creativity out of which the discipline of theology per se has been carried out since its earliest days and (2) the creative or novel aspects that now need to be "added to" the theological tradition according to the demands of the contemporary situation.[31] How, then, would we assess Yoder's understanding of constructivism and of his work as a type of "constructive theology"?

In *Practicing the Politics of Jesus*, Earl Zimmerman freely uses the language of construction to characterize Yoder's work. Zimmerman describes the latter portion of Yoder's doctoral dissertation as attempting to "sketch the outline of a constructive theology" building upon Anabaptist materials.[32] Furthermore, *Politics of Jesus* itself stands as a "radical constructive effort in theology and social ethics."[33] In Zimmerman's view, there is little question as to whether Yoder operates constructively; yet, he does suggest that Yoder lacked a sense of being "explicit" when it came to transparently characterizing the broader or systematic outlines of his project. Interestingly, though, Zimmerman doesn't explore Yoder's use of the term "construction."

Yoder's attitude toward theological construction is best exemplified by his oft-stated aversion to what he called "starting from scratch." Stanley Hauerwas cites this very phrase as the basic "error we [students of Yoder] were taught to avoid."[34] Indeed, already in *Preface to Theology*, Yoder is associating "starting from scratch" specifically with the discipline he understands as "constructive theology." As a specific type of systematic theology, theological constructivism emerges out of the mind of the single person, the one who attempts "to start over from scratch and to build one's own system in a way that has its own contemporary conviction."[35] I get the impression that for the Yoder of the late 1960s, the potential error of this constructivist approach lies in its individualism—in allowing the impulses, needs, and ego of the solitary thinker to take control of the theological process based upon "simply how one feels about everything."[36]

Later, in "Walk and Word: The Alternatives to Methodologism," Yoder contrasts the classical notion to "start from 'scratch'" with the "human social fabric" mediated by communication. Finally, in the introduction to *For the Nations*, he defends his position of refusing to start "from scratch" by arguing that such an approach signals a type of "artifice" that for his theological sensibilities fails to adequately take account of subject matter that is already "awash in debate."[37] In these cases, constructivism stands for him as a method, an "ism," a meta-position that can all-to-easily do violence to the ordinary language and common life of the discipling community.

Yet in "Thinking Theologically from a Free-Church Perspective," Yoder lifts up Paul Tillich as a positive example of theological construction. Although Tillich's work seems to claim to stand "above communities, Scriptures, and histories" as a "personal *tour de force*," his approach nevertheless represents an admirable model of an internally coherent, all-encompassing "constructive" approach to systematics that avoids many of the common ideological or even oppressive pitfalls of systematic theology-as-usual. Could a thinker in the free-church tradition take up such a project as Tillich's? It may be news to Hauerwas that Yoder answers, interestingly, that "there is no reason" why such a person "*could not* in principle take on such a 'constructive' enterprise." To be sure, Yoder notes, one must be on the lookout for the seductions of "elitism," "faddism," and, (in an apparent response to Kaufman) "the stewardship of creative energies" that such a project might engender.[38] However, he does leave the reader with an optimistic sense of the possibility of a "leaner" and "more mobile" approach to systematics, as one finds, he notes, in the occasional writings of Paul, Augustine, and Luther.[39] Free-church theological construction will give attention, above all, to the "unity of faith and life," and thus the task will "have to be done over in every other time and place."[40]

So was *Yoder* such a constructive theologian? No, in the sense that he does not label his approach as constructive in the strong sense of the word. Rather than "starting from scratch," he believes himself to be working more historically, serving to illustrate, reframe, and critique problems as they come up through the temporal development of conflicting ideas.[41] In *Preface to Theology*, for example, he understands himself and his readers to be moving "inductively, descriptively, watching the theological activity of the early Christian church, drawing our conclusions about how we ought to do theology from how it has been done in the past."[42]

Nevertheless, Yoder certainly does fit into the "stream"[43] of constructivism in Kaufman's broader, more inclusive sense of *all* theological work being "constructive." Yoder's own normative voice is unmistakably present, even in the above historical or descriptive exercises, in the way his lists are arranged and in the way that the mainstream framing of ethical debates are uncovered and exploded. Perhaps this voice does not, as he claims, constitute a method, or a system, or even a "position."[44] But there is, he says, a "tone of voice," or "style," or "stance" that the people of God exhibit,[45] and a "common *stance*" that is represented theologically in the free church tradition and in those who, with "integrity," attempt to think and write out of that tradition.[46] Even if represented by using "the concepts of others," he sees himself as nevertheless attempting to "articulate the present pertinence of my view."[47]

So Yoder does see himself as authentically entering into the project of locating, defining, and setting forth a normative vision for his tradition.

And in the process, certain key symbols and phrases are necessarily going to come to the fore for him—Jesus' politics, ecclesiology as social ethics, the victory of the Lamb, and so on. This is constructive theological work, in the sense that he is being "careful and accountable"[48] about his linguistic constructs. Furthermore, he is at the same time articulating a broader hermeneutical context, proposing a particular place to stand in relation to those words that will serve the community and guide it ethically toward, for example, its "creative response to the next confessional context,"[49] or, in relation to Christian/Jewish dialogue, its "constructive appropriation of the other's identity."[50]

Conclusion

For me, the question remains whether Yoder's tentative yet constructive suggestions are theologically robust enough to serve the very purposes he wants them to serve. Yoder's failure to consistently operate in a critical and constructive way in relation to his concept of God, one might argue, allows him to continue to traffic in the idea of God's vengeance being in some way present in the world, and in the idea of the appropriate human response being (as in the Exodus account) "to believe and obey"[51] in the face of such a theological construct. Yoder himself locates, in one passage in the *Preface*, the notion of "suspicion" as central to his concept of the task of theology.[52] And I believe he is indeed on firmer theological ground in those passages where he constructively works with a model of God as loving, thus at the same time relativizing the language of wrath or obedience. *The Original Revolution*, for example, contains the following theologically remarkable passage in the closing section of the chapter on the Sermon on the Mount:

> We do not, ultimately, love our neighbor because Jesus told us to. We love our neighbor because God is like that. It is not because Jesus told us to that we love even beyond the limits of reason and justice, even to the point of refusing to kill and being willing to suffer—but because God is like that too.[53]

Here, the concept of divine command and obedience, at least in the case of Jesus, is broken. It is not because Jesus "told us to" (i.e., mere obedience) that we are motivated to act through nonviolent love. The motivation is, evidently, the attractiveness of faithfulness to a God who acts in a similar *agape*-esque way to the love manifested in Jesus. I say "evidently" because, in this passage as in numerous others, Yoder asserts and assumes—let us even say "constructs"—a particular model of God, but he does not then go on to critically probe the issue of the diversity and value of the constructs, particularly in relation to the violence of God, that he himself has put into play.

Yoder could have been more effective theologically had he taken the constructive task of theology more seriously. The challenge for the next generation of Anabaptist-Mennonite theological thinking is to continue to work with and develop the key insights and stances in Yoder's project while at the same time having the courage to acknowledge and name the theological missteps that he makes along the way. As Mennonites, we need to consider the motto, "*Sapere Aude!*[54] Dare to think and act, theologically, for ourselves!" If we approach our task in this way, then I believe Yoder can continue to be one of the important constructive theological resources Mennonites will want to draw upon throughout the twenty-first century and beyond.

Notes

1. *The Ten Commandments* (1956), directed by Cecil B. DeMille, Act 2, Scene 13.

2. John Howard Yoder, *The Politics of Jesus*, 2nd ed. (Grand Rapids, MI: Eerdmans, 1994), 76-77.

3. Ray Gingerich, "Theological Foundations for an Ethics of Nonviolence: Was Yoder's God a Warrior?" *Mennonite Quarterly Review* 77, no. 3 (2003): 418, 435. Gingerich is expanding upon a similar "Nonviolent Jesus, Violent God?" observation made by Jack Nelson-Pallmeyer in the context of the latter's critique of Yoder, Daniel Berrigan, Thomas Merton, and Richard Horsley. See Nelson-Pallmeyer, *Jesus Against Christianity: Reclaiming the Missing Jesus* (Harrisburg: Trinity Press International, 2001), 216-21.

4. Gingerich, "Theological Foundations," 434.

5. Gingerich, "Theological Foundations," 431-32. Nelson-Pallmeyer, for his part, attributes the problem to the "uncritical approach to scripture" that he finds in Yoder, among others. See *Jesus Against Christianity*, 220.

6. Gingerich, "Theological Foundations," 426 n33.

7. Nelson-Pallmeyer, *Jesus Against Christianity*, 38-53.

8. *The Ten Commandments*, Prologue. DeMille states, "The theme of this picture is whether men ought to be ruled by God's law, or whether they

ought to be ruled by the whims of a dictator like Rameses. Are men the property of the state, or are they free souls under God? This same battle continues throughout the world today."

9. *The Ten Commandments*, Act 1, Scene 29.

10. This point is explicitly argued from the very beginning of his career, as in his 1954 essay "Peace Without Eschatology," in which in the present reign of Christ, "evil, without being blotted out, is channelized by God, in spite of itself, to serve God's purposes. . . . Vengeance is not thereby redeemed or made good; it is nonetheless rendered subservient to God's purposes" (*The Royal Priesthood* [Scottdale, PA: Herald Press, 1998], 149). At the end of his career, as well, we find him choosing to order the material in his final book, *For the Nations*, such that the final essay closes with the argument that God is free to use Assyria, Persia, or Rome for the purposes of expressing, "for ultimate good," precisely the vengeance that the followers of Jesus are called to renounce (*For the Nations: Essays Evangelical and Public* [Grand Rapids, MI: Eerdmans, 1997], 244-45). See Gingerich, "Theological Foundations," 423-24.

11. Gingerich, "Theological Foundations," 433.

12. Yoder, *For the Nations*, 85 n11. See Gingerich, "Theological Foundations," 428.

13. Gingerich, "Theological Foundations," 430.

14. Yoder, *Preface to Theology: Christology and Theological Method* (Grand Rapids, MI: Brazos Press, 2002), chapters 4 and 5.

15. Observe, for example, Hauerwas's curious equivocation on assigning the descriptor "theologian" to Yoder: "John was a theologian all the way down, but he was one with the analytical skills of the most demanding philosopher" ("Introduction: Lingering with Yoder's Wild Work," in *A Mind Patient and Untamed: Assessing John Howard Yoder's Contributions to Theology, Ethics, and Peacemaking*, ed. Ben C. Ollenburger and Gayle Gerber Koontz, [Telford, PA: Cascadia, 2004], 11), versus "Yoder . . . never understood himself to be a theologian. He often said if he had any scholarly home, it was as a historian of the left wing of the Reformation" ("Introduction," with Alex Sider, to *Preface to Theology*, 14).

16. Gordon Kaufman, *In Face of Mystery* (Cambridge, MA: Harvard University Press, 1993), chapters 6 and 7.

17. Ray Gingerich, "Resurrection: The Nonviolent Politics of God," unpublished manuscript, p. 7. On the theme in Yoder's thought of Jesus as "fully revelatory" of the image of God, see *Politics*, 101 (in this case in light of a later view of Trinity): "Christians, who believe in only one God, can affirm that he is most adequately and bindingly known in Jesus."

18. Nelson-Pallmeyer, *Jesus Against Christianity*, 228.

19. Yoder, *For the Nations*, 245.

20. Yoder, *Preface to Theology*, 44.

21. Sallie McFague, *Models of God: Theology for an Ecological, Nuclear Age* (Philadelphia: Fortress Press, 1987), 36.

22. Ibid., 63-78.

23. Yoder, "Thinking Theologically from a Free-Church Perspective," in *Doing Theology in Today's World*, ed. John D. Woodbridge and Thomas Edward McComiskey (Grand Rapids, MI: Zondervan, 1991), 259.

24. Nancey Murphy, "John Howard Yoder's Systematic Defense of Christian Pacifism," *Wisdom of the Cross: Essays in Honor of John Howard Yoder*, ed. Stanley Hauerwas, et al (Grand Rapids, MI: Eerdmans, 1999), 48. See Gingerich, "Theological Foundations," 421 n16.

25. Harry Huebner, "Moral Agency as Embodiment: How the Church Acts" in *Wisdom of the Cross*, 206.

26. Gingerich, "Theological Foundations," 435.

27. Yoder, *The Original Revolution: Essays on Christian Pacifism* (Scottdale: Herald Press, 1971, 1977), 47.

28. Yoder, *Politics of Jesus*, 238.

29. Yoder, "Introduction" to Millard Lind, *Yahweh Is a Warrior* (Scottdale: Herald Press, 1980), 19.

30. See Yoder, *For the Nations*, 9-11; Gingerich, "Theological Foundations," 417; J. Denny Weaver, *Nonviolent Atonement* (Grand Rapids, MI: Eerdmans, 2001), 457. Hauerwas, in "History, Theory, and Anabaptism: A Conversation on Theology after John Howard Yoder," states, "None of his books were attempts to develop some freestanding intellectual project" (*Wisdom of the Cross*, 391). Nancey Murphy notes that Yoder believed "theology should be written in the service of the church, addressing issues as they arise, and not driven by any philosophical or systematic motivations," but then she goes on to demonstrate "the systematic coherence of Yoder's theology" ("John Howard Yoder's Systematic Defense of Christian Pacifism," in *The Wisdom of the Cross*, 45).

31. Gordon Kaufman, *God the Problem* (Cambridge, MA: Harvard University Press, 1972), 86; *An Essay on Theological Method*, 3rd ed. (New York: Oxford University Press, 1979), chapter 2; *In Face of Mystery*, ix and chapter 3. Most recently, Kaufman has formulated his position in relation to point 1 as follows: "Theological work has always been a constructive . . . activity, engaged in imaginatively as women and men have had to come to terms with new contingencies, new issues, new problems" (*In the Beginning . . . Creativity* [Minneapolis: Fortress, 2004], 30). In relation to point 2, he writes: "In my opinion . . . Christian theology should no longer be thought of as essentially a hermeneutical task, that is, as largely interpretation of traditional materials . . . its central task is essentially constructive: to put together a Christian world-picture (or some important features of that picture) appropriate, in a

specific context, for orienting human life, reflection, and devotion" (*Jesus and Creativity* [Minneapolis: Fortress, 2006], 2).

32. Earl Zimmerman, *Practicing the Politics of Jesus: The Origin and Significance of John Howard Yoder's Social Ethics* (Telford, PA: Cascadia Publishing House, 2007), 158.

33. Ibid., 27, 185ff.

34. Stanley Hauerwas and Chris Huebner, "History, Theory, and Anabaptism," in *Wisdom of the Cross*, 407.

35. Yoder, *Preface to Theology*, 34.

36. Ibid., 43.

37. Yoder, *For the Nations*, 10. See *Royal Priesthood*, 121: "Starting from scratch with a general system and unfolding it with balance and completeness will be a rare privilege. The theologian is always 'on the way.'"

38. Yoder, "Thinking Theologically," 254-55. Kaufman, for his part, does not like the language of starting "from scratch," either: "[A]lthough I think we confront a situation unique in human history, this does not mean all past insights and knowledge are thereby overthrown, and we now must begin from scratch. Much of what I have said about human existence, about the mystery in which life is ensconced, about finitude and contingency, is of course rooted in traditional religious and philosophical reflection. But in our time those roots are bringing forth a new flower—if it is a flower—namely a new and profounder awareness both of the extent of human power and the enormous threat of contingency, thus contributing to a new sense of the ultimate mystery at the center of human life." See *Theology for a Nuclear Age* (Manchester: Manchester University Press, 1985), 13-14.

39. Yoder, "Thinking Theologically," 254.

40. Ibid., 256.

41. This is evident in the way he looks at various approaches to, for example, the social ethics of Jesus in the biblical text (*The Politics of Jesus*), the growth of early Christian theology and ecclesiology (*Preface to Theology*), the articulation and practice of religious pacifism (*Nevertheless*), and foundational starting points for ethical reflection ("Walk and Word").

42. Yoder, *Preface to Theology*, 39.

43. Yoder develops the metaphor of the theological tradition as a "stream" in *Preface to Theology*, 382-83.

44. Hauerwas, "Introduction: Lingering with Yoder's Wild Work," in *A Mind Patient and Untamed*, 11, writes: "[Yoder] realized that what he cared about could not be considered just 'another position.'"

45. Yoder, *For the Nations*, 1.

46. Yoder, "Thinking Theologically," 251, and *For the Nations*, 10.

47. Yoder, "Patience as a Method in Moral Reasoning," in *The Wisdom of the Cross*, 28.

48. Yoder, *Preface to Theology*, 44; see *Royal Priesthood*, 140: "To do theology, the proverb said, is to be careful about one's words in the fear of God."

49. Yoder, *Royal Priesthood*, 121.

50. Yoder, *The Jewish-Christian Schism Revisited* (Grand Rapids, MI: Eerdmans, 2003), 115.

51. Yoder, *Politics of Jesus*, 77; see Yoder's letter to J. Lawrence Burkholder, June 12, 1956, as quoted by Zimmerman, *Practicing the Politics of Jesus*, 107.

52. Yoder, *Preface to Theology*, 395.

53. Yoder, *The Original Revolution*, 51.

54. See Immanuel Kant, "An Answer to the Question: What is Enlightenment?" in *Perpetual Peace and Other Essays* (Indianapolis: Hackett, 1983), 41.

Chapter 3

The Practice of Reading the Other:
John Howard Yoder's Critical and Caricatured Portrayal of Scholasticism

Andrew Brubacher Kaethler

I especially do not give scholastic traditions the benefit of the doubt, when one can see that those by whom they were articulated in history were the defenders of specific interests distinguishable from the Kingdom of God.
—John Howard Yoder[1]

John Howard Yoder is with most Protestant and many Catholic ethicists and theologians in the twentieth- and twenty-first centuries who also "do not give scholastic traditions the benefit of the doubt." What is surprising, nevertheless, is that for a theologian who claims "patience" as method, who seeks to fully understand his dialogue partner, and who seeks "ecumenical" dialogue, Yoder readily dismisses scholasticism. This essay will first appreciatively observe Yoder's engagement with scholasticism around just war theory and around biblical authority and interpretation. The essay will then demonstrate that Yoder oversimplifies his portrayal of scholasticism, unfairly pegging it as irredeemably wedged between the competing "Constantinian" methodologisms of "Rome" and "reason." The essay will conclude by utilizing sources from within Yoder's own writings to suggest how Yoder may have engaged scholasticism more patiently and how postmodern theologians may interact with modern and premodern theology.

Scholasticism in this essay refers broadly to scholastic method and themes prevalent in the late medieval and early modern periods but having a subtle lingering presence to this day. Since Yoder sees scholasticism as instances and expressions of Constantinianism, this essay will maintain focus on the areas of discussion Yoder initiates. *Methodologism* is Yoder's term for any amount of allegiance to methods, theories, and systems. Such allegiance invariably precludes consideration of a wide variety of particular perspectives, approaches, and interests that may be more in keeping with the kingdom of God than the dominant, universalizing, and totalizing Constantinian perspectives, approaches, and interests methodology tends to support.

Part 1—References and Themes

Medieval and High Protestant Scholasticism

While Yoder identifies different incarnations of scholasticism throughout the centuries, he maintains that they all conserve a Constantinian vision of how one is expected to act within the "realities" of a given social order. Yoder's central objective in his writing on scholasticism is to demonstrate the ongoing, sweeping, and deleterious effects of the Constantinian turn and to disclose the methodological machinery necessary to perpetuate Constantinianism. "[T]he medieval legend which made of Constantine the symbol of an epochal shift was realistic: he stands for a new era in the history of Christianity."[2] This new era is still with us, periodically reinventing itself for more than a millennium and a half in "neo-Constantinianisms."[3]

The most informative setting in which Yoder addresses medieval scholasticism is in relation to just war thinking. In *Christian Attitudes to War, Peace, and Revolution*[4] Yoder engages Thomas Aquinas in discussion on just war from the *Summa theologiae* 2.2 Question 40. Aquinas lays out three conditions for just war: war must be declared by a sovereign ruler (not an individual), it must have just cause, and it must further a good.[5] Yoder accepts that these conditions do not constitute "blanket approval" and demonstrate a significant emphasis on restraint.[6] But according to Yoder, the limited restraint that Aquinas affords is overshadowed in the following article of the *Summa*, in which clergy are explicitly prohibited from participating in war because it would be "unbecoming of them to slay or shed blood." Priests should only be willing to shed their own blood in order to "imitate what they portray in their ministry,"[7] that is, the ministry of the Eucharist. This logic was still in effect centuries later as men preparing for the priesthood were excused from participating in the trial of Michael Sattler in 1527 lest as jury members they would decide in favor of death as the penalty.[8] Yoder concludes that scholastic logic is deficient because killing is held as a "permanent moral blemish" yet is deemed ethically "justifiable" and forgivable.[9]

Yoder therefore questions the integrity of scholastic reasoning on both pragmatic and logical grounds. Pragmatic issues include: that priests have little direct input into the state's decision to go to war; that neither priests nor princes have cogent theories of justice; that soldiers are not considered independent moral agents; that the priest's primary context for moral discernment is after the fact, during confession, when the priest hears out the penitent's sins and decides on the appropriate acts of penance before they can participate in the Eucharist again;[10] and that since the Eucharist is never permanently withheld, the church has little hard recourse to limit killing.

The logical limits to scholastic reasoning are equally weighty. Yoder maintains that Aquinas's systematization of thought lacks a "coherent *intellectual* system" or a "formal *operational* statement." Aquinas creates "rather the kind of list you have in a dictionary or an encyclopedia,"[11] "making *assumptions* that moral reasoning as a whole goes on as before about one question, namely truth telling, in a way that has been abandoned about the other question, killing."[12] Simultaneously, Aquinas assumes a unified culture in which "common sense" and consensus are pervasive and the church-world distinction is collapsed. For all the rigor of scholasticism, its deliberation is incomplete.[13] In short, Yoder finds it problematic that Aquinas's system is internally incoherent yet externally generalized and that the existence of the church is so inextricably bound up with the existence of the state that the integrity of the church's witness to the state is compromised.

A second setting in which Yoder addresses medieval scholasticism is in relation to "reality" and the social order.[14] Yoder appreciates how scholastics such as Aquinas seek to keep nature and grace together in a "complimentary and organic way" but he laments that "the nature of things" is confined to "the way things are now in the fallen world, especially in ethnic and national definitions of community and patriarchal definitions of order."[15] By contrast, the prophetic community "affirms 'the nature of

things' more profoundly than the scholastic vision because it reads the substantial definition of nature from the incarnation and holy history, not
from medieval culture *or* Greek philosophy."[16] Medieval scholastics give
priority to Greek ontology over an incarnational ontology, the latter being
"the restored vision for how things really are."[17]

Yoder concludes that Aquinas and medieval scholasticism generally are
stuck between Rome and reason, between serving the state and serving an
intellectual system. They box reality into one "seamless"[18] but fallen system
that is ineffective in challenging Constantinian interests and represses a messianic or incarnational view of the world.

The critiques Yoder levels against scholasticism in the post-Reformation
era revolve around the Enlightenment quest for epistemological foundationalism.[19] Yoder traces contemporary problems in epistemology and biblical
interpretation backwards through High Modernity (HM), High Protestant
Scholasticism (HPS), and High Tridentine Catholic (HTC). HPS often
claimed it escaped the tension between "Rome and 'reason'" by relying on
Scripture alone, while HTC conceded too much to tradition (Rome) and
HM conceded too much to biblical-historical criticism.

To highlight Yoder's response to just one of these expressions of foundationalism, Yoder rebuffs HPS's insistence on the uniqueness of Scripture.
"In all its consistency and solidity [it] does not make sense standing alone.
It could not have grown directly out of the Bible." The very trap HPS is
trying to avoid, human explanation as the foundation, is reified along with
the canon. That God intends the canon be given priority over other sacred
writings; that the process of canonization itself is divinely inspired; and
that God has guarded or preserved the canon through the centuries, these
are all about human history and are all extrabiblical.[20] The "miraculous"[21]
nature of canonization and the ahistorical, systematic organization of biblical truths are merely concessions to "the culture of the Protestant
Scholastic movement."[22] Yoder decries the loss of historical particularity
that is bound to the "HTC/HPS/HM heritage," not only of Jesus and the
original writers of the Scriptures but also for readers today. He maintains
that while the canon *does* allow the church to embrace diversity while
maintaining a norming process, rather than assume with modernism that
pluralism ends norms or with "orthodoxy" that norms end pluralism, this
process occurs outside foundational impulses.[23]

Scholasticism, whether pre- or post-Reformation, defends and ratifies
prevalent social structures against gospel criticisms. It concedes biblical

interpretation to dominant cultural epistemology, be it to Greek/Aristotelian reason in the late medieval period or to Enlightenment reason in the modern period.[24] Scholasticism disallows "testing" Scripture, reduces dynamic and diverse ways of interpreting the gospel to codifications, systems, theories, and the priority of style, and ensconces totalizing "methodologism."[25]

Ontology, Natural Theology, and Analogy

Ontology, natural theology and analogy are three interrelated themes central to scholasticism. Yoder critically appraises all three.

Yoder is extremely cautious when using the term *ontology*. He treats it with stern suspicion when it is used to denote the metaphysical concept of "being" or to make a priori pronouncements on reality and truth claims about "the way things are" separated from christological claims. For instance, regarding Gotthold Lessing's "solid ground beyond the ditch," where one might expect to find a secure, objective, pan-optic perch, Yoder writes:

> [It] is not there. The less narrow truth over there is still also provincial. Reality always was pluralistic and relativistic, that is, historical. The idea that it could be otherwise was itself an illusion laid on us by Greek ontology language, Roman sovereignty language, and other borrowings from the Germans, the Moors, and the other rulers of Europe.[26]

There is only this side where a particular community is shaped by the biblical narrative.[27] Yet Yoder is willing to talk about the ontology of the good news when it points toward new and in-breaking forms of existence, of an "ontological decision, dictated by a truer picture of what the world *really is*."[28] As Yoder writes in *Politics of Jesus*, the "accent lies not on transforming the ontology of the person . . . but on transforming the perspective of one who has accepted Christ as his context."[29] In other words, there is no change in the structure of one's "being," only in how one views the world and the commitments one makes in living in this world.

The key to Yoder's selective use of ontology may in fact be found in his critique of *natural theology*. Yoder is concerned that any appeal to the way things are in nature is usually an attempt to epistemologically circumvent the Scriptures in favor of "wider wisdom" and "common sense,"[30] (Yoder's terms for anthropological reductionism and autonomous human reasoning). Yoder writes, "The reason I do not trust claims to 'natural insight' is that the dominant moral view of any *known* world are oppressive, provincial, or to say it theologically, 'fallen.'"[31] The problem with an epistemology that is based on "the way things are" or "the nature of things," then, is precisely that it is void of eschatological or kingdom considerations. As with Yoder's redefinition of ontology, he argues for a view of the created, natural order that embraces the "vision" of those who confess Jesus Christ as Lord have the responsibility to "see" and "observe" in a particular way that is not shackled by fallen realities. It is only with this redeemed way of seeing that events like the cross make sense: "The cross is neither foolish nor weak, but natural."[32]

The final scholastic concept to be considered is *analogy*. Analogy had faded as a theological concept of significant importance by the twentieth century, maintained primarily by some Catholic theologians. But Karl Barth feared the notion of *analogia entis* was poised for a revival in Protestant theology and vehemently declared "no" to the theological possibilities of the analogy of being, referring provocatively to it as "an invention of the anti-Christ."[33] Yoder, following Barth, recognizes that the *analogia entis* factored prominently in the development of natural theology.

However, Yoder decries the "exploratory whimsicality" with which Barth employs analogy in other areas.[34] The point here is not to establish the degree or manner in which Barth, as a Reformed or neo-orthodox theologian, displays vestiges of scholastic themes and method. Rather, it is to illustrate Yoder's sensitivity to analogy, even as it creeps unsuspectingly into the work of his respected teacher. Yoder distinguishes between being able to illustrate something and being able to establish something as true or normative. He laments that Barth's "undisciplined" use of analogy compromises the ability of the church to constitute "the backbone of social ethics" because ecclesiastical function is reduced to a mode of communication instead of as the "first fruits" of the kingdom.[35]

The primary example Yoder offers for the serious limits of analogy, then, are in Barth's discussion of *Grenzfall*, the "borderline case." Because analogy is imprecise, Yoder feels it allows Barth to do two things "completely 'non-Barthian.'" It allows the command of God, in this case, "Thou shalt not kill," to be reduced to a general principle, and it allows Barth to ignore the "Word of God spoken to the situation" in favor of considering only the "bare situation"[36] (Barth's own example is the hypothetical case regarding the response of Christians in Switzerland should

Nazi Germany attack).[37] Yoder argues that although Barth categorically excludes casuistry as a valid form of theological and ethical inquiry into proper human action in response to God's commands,[38] Barth's use of analogy here opens the door to casuistry and compromises the church's witness regarding the Lordship of Christ.[39] The logic of analogy is problematic because it is Constantinian in its "generalizability," excluding "faith and unbelief as significant variables."[40] Analogy strips faith of particularity in expression.

The Emerging View

The view that emerges from part 1 is that Yoder paints a consistent, though unnuanced, picture of scholasticism. The threads that in Yoder's view unite scholasticism through the centuries are: (1) a desire for social unity concurrent with (2) a belief in the universalizability of method (methodological Constantinianism) and the generalizability of conclusions (univocal pronouncements) (3) through appeal to dominant contemporary "culture" over Scripture (named, as with Aquinas, and unnamed, as with High Protestant Scholasticism), (4) coming at the expense of the plurality, diversity, and particularity of Christian existence and (5) permitting unchallenged appeals to "common sense" and assumptions regarding reality (6) that are based more on the fallen state of the world than on a kingdom vision of reality. Yoder seeks less to understand scholasticism as a dialogue partner and more to simply wipe the table of scholastic reasoning. Occasionally he employs "middle axioms" to hold others accountable within their own system of thought, but Yoder's ultimate goal is to dismiss or transcend the position of the other as inadequate.[41]

Part 2—A Critical Evaluation of Yoder's Caricature

To charge Yoder of caricature is serious given Yoder's own frustration with how the Radical Reformation and free church movements have been caricatured by others. He complains, for example, that Ernst Troeltsch and the Niebuhrs oversimplify radical discipleship movements by suggesting minority discipleship simply abjure society. "That discipleship means social withdrawal is a caricature projected by Troeltsch and the Niebuhrs, on grounds related to their own assumptions, not drawn from historical facts."[42] It would seem, then, that one would need to evaluate the degree to which Yoder is doing this very thing and the degree to which he misreads scholasticism and disregards the "historical facts."

Yoder's Use of Caricature

Yoder himself uses the term *caricature*. Sometimes it conveys negative connotations (as above) and sometimes neutral or positive connotations, as when he acknowledges the "simplicity of caricature."[43] The problem is not that he uses the term both positively and negatively, but that when he uses it as a positive term he is generally doing something similar to what he laments his opponents do when they use it. Yoder's caricature of scholasticism for the sake of simplicity is methodologically indistinguishable from Troeltsch's caricature of Anabaptism as sect in his three-fold typology of forms of Christian community. By leaving out details regarding scholasticism Yoder not only perpetuates common superficial depictions (e.g. that scholastic theology is "immature," "external," "ritualistic," "wooden")[44] but also collapses scholasticism into Constantinianism. Scholasticism, thinly defined, bears the brunt of what he demurs about the development of just war thinking and biblical interpretation.

In a similarly oversimplified manner, Aquinas is selected as *the* representative of medieval scholasticism and other prominent scholastics are ignored. One wonders if Yoder might find a better medieval sparing partner in Duns Scotus, who derives a "univocity of being" from *analogia entis* and whose immanentist ontology displaces particularity of knowledge and existence with the universality of reason and a "pervasive meaning system."[45] Yoder's oversimplified, unnuanced caricature of scholasticism is itself a kind of totalizing, universalized, and generalized portrayal and a denial of historical and contextual particularity.

Non-Constantinian Possibilities in Aquinas's Use of Scripture

In oversimplifying Aquinas's writings and granting him too great a voice in the medieval church, Yoder perpetuates the widely held but inaccurate perception that scholastic method relies predominantly on extrabiblical sources of knowledge such as Greek philosophy and other "'cultural' epistemologies." Yoder downplays Aquinas's extensive use of Scripture in order to build the case that Aquinas shares "specific interests distinguishable from the Kingdom of God."[46] The misconception that medieval scholastics in general, and Aquinas in particular, mute Scripture by either ignoring it or by reducing it to one "voice" is challenged by Stephen Fowl.[47] Fowl notes that in the *Summa theologiae* there are on average five-and-a-half scriptural quotations per one thousand words and that Scripture is quoted far more than any other source. To say that Aquinas is a theologian is certainly to say he is a *biblical* theologian.[48]

Fowl further confronts the assumption that scholastic method is formulaic and that Aquinas's method relies on a "general hermeneutic" that only leads to a single, "literal" reading of a text, speaking to Yoder's claim that Aquinas falls lock-step into the Constantinian stress on unifying culture, "common sense," and generalizability. Fowl, however, contends that since Aquinas defines "literal" as the sense in which the author intends and that he defines the author as the Holy Spirit, multiple meanings are acceptable and even desirable.[49] Aquinas states in *De potentia*, "One 'should not confine the meaning of a passage of Scripture under one sense so as to exclude any other interpretations that are actually or possibly true that do not violate the context.'"[50] Aquinas affords Scripture a central role in Christian life, and recognizing that the world is complex, "a multifaceted literal sense of Scripture will be a much more successful way of comprehending God, the world, others, and all that falls between."[51] In contrast to Yoder's portrayal of Aquinas as a defender of "specific interests distinguishable from the Kingdom of God," Fowl avers that Aquinas "see[s] Scripture and its interpretation, not as an end in itself, but as a central way in which God draws us into ever deeper friendship. Further, rather than providing a set of proof texts for doctrine, we should study, interpret and engage Scripture to deepen and enrich the agreements between Scripture and our doctrine, faith and practice."[52]

Non-Constantinian Possibilities in Protestant Scholasticism

On this side of the Reformation, Yoder implicates Protestant scholasticism with foundationalist Enlightenment thinking. But Luco J. van den Brom suggests that scholastic method does not necessarily lead to ahistorical theology. Van den Brom takes Barth's comments that "Abhorrence of scholasticism is the mark of the false prophet" and "A true [prophet] will, in the final analysis, be prepared to submit his message also to this [scholastic] test"[53] to mean that one does not need to fear scholasticism for its method. Van den Brom contends that the aim of scholasticism was never to develop a life of its own but to render a contemporary understanding of Scripture.[54] While Yoder shares Barth's aversion to natural theology, Barth is more open than Yoder to acknowledge that natural theology is not the only, or necessary, outcome of scholasticism. Barth's dialectic theology certainly bears marks of scholastic method. Van den Brom then goes on to show how the "Utrecht school" in the Netherlands has in recent decades developed an interest in scholastic method and has used it to develop a dynamic theology that emphasizes the personal and relational attributes of God and a vibrant Trinitarian theology.[55]

Is Yoder opposed to method per se? Chris Huebner reads Yoder to suggest that theories, methods, and systems themselves naturally lead to epistemological violence, especially when they are detached from the practicing community. Huebner suggests Yoder stops short of making an explicit commitment to "anti-" positions (anti-theory, anti-system, anti-method) because he does not want to turn them into another form of Constantinian methodologism.[56] It is telling, however, that Huebner can talk only of Yoder's epistemological pacifism, not methodological pacifism, or that Yoder can talk about "patience as method" but can only talk about different kinds of patience, not different kinds of method.[57] A careful reading of Yoder reveals that he is not against method and system per se, but against any one method, including anti-method method, becoming dominant.[58] But this leaves some unaddressed issues.

One issue that needs to be addressed is how Yoder connects methodologism with monologism, that is, with univocal, totalizing pronouncements? Is the relationship causal or coincidental? We can only presume that Yoder is intentionally silent on this issue and that causality is implied. Another issue is why scholastic method is systematically rejected as one of many systems employed. In order to maintain that scholastic systems and methods are "unfaithful," promoting ahistoric and inflexible interpretations of the gospel that benefit the system-makers,[59] a Yoderian response needs to at least address the counterpoints articulated by the likes of Fowl and van den Brom, who demonstrate the dialogical and multilayered nature of scholastic thought and biblical interpretation.

If the "burden of proof" needs to lie with the methodologists, let it be so. If pluralism in epistemological method is "good news," then scholastic method should not be excluded. Comments like the following should be less exceptional and applied more broadly: "For some purposes Aquinas's claim to contain everything under one tent in the name of Aristotle may be appropriate; in others it is both silly and presumptuous."[60] What is needed is this same admission for the potential appropriateness of Aquinas's claims to be more fully integrated into all his writings on scholasticism. Without this his portrayal of scholasticism remains a caricature.

Part 3—Lessons for Engaging Premodern and Modern Theology in Postmodernity

Finally, we turn to Yoder himself to offer suggestions for a more "patient" interpretation of scholasticism. Of the six lessons below, four are derived from the essay, "'Patience' as Method in Moral Reasoning: Is an Ethic of Discipleship 'Absolute'?"[61] Two are derived from other works of Yoder. Not only are there implications herein that apply to Yoder's treatment of scholasticism, but these implications apply more broadly to any postmodern readings of premodern and modern theology.

Is Yoder a postmodern theologian? Yoder did not use the label "postmodern" to describe himself. In the sense that he refuses to set the epistemological and ecclesiological stage in a Cartesian theatre[62] and repudiates foundationalist, objectivist, and totalizing theological claims he is in the company of many postmodern theologians. In the sense that he privileges certain postmodern postcritical methodologies over others, he is not. Nevertheless, because Yoder seeks both the particularity and continuity of the church and claim avows a pacifist epistemology that asserts "Jesus is Lord" as a non-totalizing ontological claim, his theology has significant import for theology and the church in postmodernity.

The overarching lesson is that caricature is unhelpful and methodologically impatient. It readily slips from being a handy pedagogical tool that untangles messy details from the main point or collective effect into a reductionist and totalizing position. Caricature positions Yoder too close to epistemological foundationalism and methodologism and farther from the pacifist epistemology and methodological patience he advocates. Caricature is especially problematic for postmodern theology where nuance and subtlety are valued as expressions of particularity. P. Travis Kroeker is thus right in suggesting that Yoder's dichotomy between Jewish and Greek Christianity is too neat and convenient and sets a polarizing tone for his genealogical critique of Constantinianism. Yoder would do well to attend to the complex and variegated relationship between Jewish and Greek Christianity, as well as be more open to valuing "gifts and treasures" from Platonic philosophy.[63] The same can be said about avoiding too-sharp distinctions between Thomistic-Aristotelean theology and radical reformation movements, and about accepting the gifts and treasures of that classical tradition.

A second lesson originates from what Yoder terms "corrective" patience. An example of corrective patience is the way sixteenth-century Protestantism appealed to "The Scriptures" in a way that was needed to correct medieval Christianity, even though "when systematized it became wooden and epistemologically naïve." Protestant reformers served a dialogical role and appropriately formed their challenges to medieval expressions of Constantinian Christianity from their contexts.[64] The same logic applies in positing that medieval scholasticism offers dialogical and contextual "correctives" to Late Antiquity. Yoder himself contends, "There are valid points needing to be made whose validity should not be negated on the ground that in a given setting the only way available to make them is subject to criticism from some other level."[65] This comment clears space for critically appreciating scholastic dialogue partners such as Aquinas on their own terms. Corrective patience must equally apply to postmodern critiques of modern theology. For instance, in evaluating the wedge Kant drives between faith and reason in the pursuit for certainty of knowledge, one needs to leave ample space for appreciating his context and the complexities of the issues.

Third, Yoder claims at times to use "multicultural patience."[66] While he likely was thinking more about contemporary cultures than historic ones, I suggest the same patience should apply to scholastic culture. Cultures extend across time as well as space; historic cultures, perhaps even eras such as modernity, deserve the same patience as different contemporary cultures. Yoder employs multicultural patience with Judaism and medieval Christianity deserves the same.

Yoder claims to resist the "drive . . . for a single master method." This fourth kind of patience requires one to "meeting the interlocutor on his own terms," rather than, for example, "sweepingly denouncing casuistry as do Karl Barth, Jacques Ellul, and some Lutherans."[67] One wonders if prohibitions against sweeping pronouncements should apply to the quote at the top of this essay. Further, there is something instructive to be learned by Yoder's mention of Barth here. Barth, who states categorically that casuistry is not a valid method of ethical discernment, is criticized by Yoder for succumbing to causistry when Barth considers what an appropriate Christian response should be in the hypothetical scenario of Nazi

Germany attacking Switzerland.[68] Yoder has the opposite problem. While he normally argues that many methods should be considered to avoid absolutism, here, where he is arguing for patience with the interlocutor, rules out casuistry in a rather "impatient" and "bellicose"[69] manner.

Applied to postmodern theology, the lesson or implication of "meeting the interlocutor on his own terms" means not equating or reducing a dialogue partner to a school of thought or an era. Avoiding the drive for a master narrative in postmodernity requires that modern and premodern theologians and philosophers are not forced into what now appear to be the master narratives of their times but are allowed to speak on their own terms.

Fifth, postmodern thinkers must embrace a *particular* particularity and a *particular* pluralism. Postmodern thinkers do not need to be convinced of particularity and pluralism; these are already central to defining *postmodern*. What Yoder brings to light is that not only does the modern impulse toward universalism and homogeneity operate part-in-parcel with the drive for a master narrative, but the drive for a master narrative can also be found in postmodern thinking, in "pure particularity" or what Yoder calls "absolute relativism." Absolute relativism becomes a master narrative because it demands allegiance.[70] What is needed in postmodern theology is the concession of just one universal: the particularity of Jesus Christ. Yoder's claim that the only universal is the "nonterritorial particularity" of Jesus Christ in the incarnation[71] must surely be counted among the most important affirmations of the postmodern church, for it prevents the lapse of pluralism from relative relativity or relative pluralism into absolute relativity or absolute pluralism.

Jonathan Wilson joins Yoder in affirming that cultural and epistemological pluralism are neither new nor problematic. Pluralism existed in Enlightenment Europe and in Constantinian Rome, though suppressed at times by the drive for homogeneity and universalism. Wilson clarifies that the crisis of our age is fragmentation,[72] which results not from relative relativism but from absolute relativism. Pluralism as relative relativism accepts Babel as a gift to the human condition, saving humanity from the idolatry of self-divinization and providing the means for transmission of the good news. Babel is the way God intends things to be, even before the story of Babel itself. Absolute relativism and universalism are two sides of the same coin and both "babble." Both assume a "common ground" language, a "prior" or "higher" level of communication.[73] The incarnation is an affirmation of pluralism as relative relativism. The particularity of Christ is an affront to universalism and absolute relativism. Contra the entrenchment of absolute relativism, the incarnation represents a nonterritorial particularity; contra universalism, a nontotalizing proclamation of the good news.

Hence, absolute relativity and fragmentation also inhibit our ability to engage in ecumenical dialogue because everyone is befuddled by babble. But when the particularity of each worshipping community is valued, true ecumenism is possible. Where Scripture-reading communities converse with one another and challenge one another a more faithful reading and living of the Gospel is discovered. In the words of Nancey Murphy and Brad Kallenberg, "When *this* community rightly reads Scripture, its reading takes the form of ecumenical conversation that is sometimes reforming and other times prophetic."[74]

Finally, a lesson for postmodern theology is to maintain a non-neurotic suspicion of foundationalism and a humble epistemology. This requires consciously avoiding the tendencies to either drift back to modernity in the quest for certainty and a firm foundation of knowledge or to drift with deconstructionism and absolute relativism toward nihilism. It is curious that Yoder, who himself adopted a kind of premodern precritical biblical realist stance toward reading and interpreting the Scriptures, so readily dismisses the one thousand years of precritical interpretation before the Reformation. Stanley Hauerwas highlights a good example of Yoder's precritical approach when he notes that Yoder's statement about the slain Lamb, that "people who bear crosses are working with the grain of the universe," is not so much a confessional statement but a "metaphysical claim about the way things are."[75] Yoder's pacifist ethics are grounded in a pacifist epistemology that simply sees "bearing crosses" as the way things are and should be. The Christian's nonneurotic suspicion of foundationalism and humble epistemology suggest that Christian hope is not to be found in a past Eden or a future universal church, and not in the overcoming of time and death altogether, but in the way of the cross as lived by the faithful, local church.

Notes

1. John Howard Yoder, *To Hear the Word* (Eugene, OR: Wipf & Stock, 2001), 60.

2. John Howard Yoder, *The Priestly Kingdom* (Notre Dame, IN: University of Notre Dame Press, 1984), 135.

3. John Howard Yoder, *The Royal Priesthood: Essays Ecclesiological and Ecumenical*, ed. Michael Cartwright (Grand Rapids, MI: Eerdmans, 1994), 195-97.

4. John Howard Yoder, *Christian Attitudes to War, Peace, and Revolution: A Companion to Bainton* (Elkhart, IN: Peace Resource Center, 1983).

5. Thomas Aquinas, *Summa theologiae* 2.2, Question 40, Article 2, trans. Fathers of English Dominican Province, 2nd and rev. ed., 1920, http://www.newadvent.org/summa/. Accessed June 24, 2008.

6. Yoder, *Christian Attitudes to War, Peace, and Revolution*, 62.

7. See Aquinas, *Summa theologiae* 2.2, Question 40, Article 2.

8. Yoder, *Christian Attitudes to War, Peace, and Revolution*, 63.

9. Ibid., 62.

10. Ibid., 63-64.

11. Ibid., 46.

12. Ibid., 52. Italics added.

13. Ibid., 52-53.

14. John Howard Yoder, *For the Nations: Essays Public and Evangelical* (Grand Rapids, MI: Eerdmans, 1997), 199-218.

15. Ibid., 212.

16. Ibid., 214.

17. Ibid., 212.

18. Yoder, *The Priestly Kingdom*, 56.

19. Yoder, *To Hear the Word*, 60.

20. Ibid., 87. See also Yoder, *For the Nations*, 81; Williston Walker, *A History of the Christian Church* (New York: Scribner, 1959), 87.

21. Yoder, *For the Nations*, 55.

22. Yoder, *To Hear the Word*, 88.

23. Ibid., 102.

24. Ibid., 60-61.

25. Ibid., 62-65; John Howard Yoder, "Walk and Word: Alternatives to Methodologism" in *Theology Without Foundations*, ed. Stanley Hauerwas, Nancey Murphy and Mark Nation (Nashville: Abingdon Press, 1994), 77-90.

26. Yoder, *The Priestly Kingdom*, 59.

27. Yoder, *For the Nations*, 83-84.

28. Ibid, 211.

29. John Howard Yoder, *The Politics of Jesus*, 2nd ed. (Grand Rapids, MI: Eerdmans, 1994), 223.

30. Yoder, *Priestly Kingdom*, 72-73; Yoder, *For the Nations*, 20.

31. Yoder, *Priestly Kingdom*, 40.

32. Yoder, *For the Nations*, 212.

33. Karl Barth, *Church Dogmatics* (Edinburgh: T & T Clark, 1936-1975), I.1, x. Stanley Hauerwas contends that Barth softened his attack on

the *analogia entis* over the course of writing *Church Dogmatics*, developing an implied natural theology in his "Christological recovery" of theology. See Stanley Hauerwas, *With the Grain of the Universe: The Church's Witness and Natural Theology* (Grand Rapids, MI: Brazos Press, 2001), 141, 158-71.

34. Yoder, *Royal Priesthood*, 125. See Karl Barth, "The Christian Community and the Civil Community," in *Community, State and Church*, introduction by Will Herberg (Garden City, NY: Anchor Books, 1960), 149-89; Barth, *Church Dogmatics* IV.2, 719-26.

35. John Howard Yoder, *Karl Barth and the Problem of War and Other Essays on Barth*, ed. Mark Thiessen Nation (Eugene, OR: Cascade Books, 2003), 76; Yoder, *Royal Priesthood*, 125-26.

36. Yoder, *Karl Barth and the Problem of War*, 84-85.

37. Barth, *Church Dogmatics* III.4, 462.

38. See Barth, *Church Dogmatics* II.2, 661-708 and III.4, 6-15; Nigel Biggar, *The Hastening that Waits: Karl Barth's Ethics* (New York: Oxford University Press, 1993), 40-41.

39. Yoder, *For the Nations*, 24.

40. Yoder, *The Priestly Kingdom*, 151-71.

41. John Howard Yoder, *The Christian Witness to the State* (Scottdale, PA: Herald Press, 2002), 71-73.

42. Yoder, *Priestly Kingdom*, 11.

43. Yoder, *For the Nations*, 214.

44. Yoder, *Christian Attitudes to War, Peace, and Revolution*, 159. In *Politics of Jesus*, 173, n25, Yoder says High Protestant Scholasticism exhibits qualities of "uncritical woodenness" regarding "certain traditional interpretations" of Pauline attitudes toward the role of women in the church."

45. Yoder, *Priestly Kingdom*, 56.

46. Yoder, *To Hear the Word*, 60.

47. Stephen Fowl, "The Importance of a Multivoiced Literal Sense of Scripture: The Example of Thomas Aquinas," in *Reading Scripture with the Church: Toward a Hermeneutic for Theological Interpretation*, A. K. M. Adam, Stephen Fowl, Kevin J. Vanhoozer, and Francis Watson (Grand Rapids, MI: Baker Academic, 2006), 35-50.

48. Ibid., 38-39. Statistical reference in Fowl from Wilhelmus G. B. M. Valkenberg, *Words of the Living God: Place and Function of Holy Scripture in the Theology of St. Thomas Aquinas* (Leuven: Peeters, 2000), 75.

49. Fowl, "Multivoiced Literal Sense," 40-41; Aquinas, *Summa theologiae* 1.1 Question 1, Article 10, http://www.newadvent.org/summa/ 1001.htm#10. Accessed December 6, 2006.

50. Aquinas, *De potentia* Question 4.1 quote from Fowl, "Multivoiced Literal Sense," 44.

51. Fowl, "Multivoiced Literal Sense," 46-47.

52. Ibid., 50.

53. Luco J. van den Brom, "Scholasticism and Contemporary Systematic Theology," *Reformation and Scholasticism: An Ecumenical Enterprise*, eds. Willelm J. van Asselt and Eef Dekker (Grand Rapids, MI: Baker Academic, 2001), 279. Karl Barth quote from *Die Kirchliche Dogmatik* I.1 (München: C. Kaiser, 1932), 296.

54. Van den Brom, "Scholasticism," 90.

55. Ibid., 90-93.

56. Chris K. Huebner, *A Precarious Peace: Yoderian Explorations on Theology, Knowledge, and Identity* (Waterloo, ON: Herald Press, 2006), 49-68, 97-113.

57. John Howard Yoder, "'Patience' as Method in Moral Reasoning: Is an Ethic of Discipleship 'Absolute'?" in *The Wisdom of the Cross: Essays in Honor of John Howard Yoder*, ed. Stanley Hauerwas, Chris K. Huebner, Harry J. Huebner and Mark Thiessen Nation (Grand Rapids, MI: Eerdmans, 1999), 24-42.

58. Yoder, "Walk and Word," 77-90; John Howard Yoder, "Thinking Theologically from a Free-Church Perspective," in *Doing Theology in Today's World: Essays in Honor of Kenneth S. Kantzer*, ed. John D Woodbridge and Thomas Edward McComiskey (Grand Rapids, MI: Zondervan, 1991), 252.

59. Yoder, "Thinking Theologically from a Free-Church Perspective," 254.

60. Yoder, "Walk and Word," 82, 83.

61. Yoder, "'Patience' as Method in Moral Reasoning," 24-42.

62. Nancey K. Murphy and Brad K. Kallenberg, "Anglo-American Postmodernity: A Theology of Communal Practice," in *The Cambridge Companion to Postmodern Theology*, ed. Kevin J. Vanhoozer (Cambridge: Cambridge University Press, 2003), 36-39.

63. P. Travis Kroeker, "The War of the Lamb: Postmodernity and John Howard Yoder's Eschatological Genealogy of Morals," *Mennonite Quarterly Review* 74, no. 2 (2000): 295-310.

64. Yoder, "'Patience' as Method in Moral Reasoning," 26.

65. Ibid., 27.

66. Ibid., 28.

67. Ibid., 28-29.

68. Yoder, *Karl Barth and the Problem of War*, 40-89 passim.

69. Albert J. Meyer, in a letter of personal correspondence, "Karl Barth and John Yoder on the Bruderholz," September 18, 2006, personally recounts Barth's initial response to Yoder after reading for the first time the essay that would become the book, *Karl Barth and the Problem of War*, accusing Yoder

of being "bellicose."

70. John Howard Yoder, "Meaning after Babble: With Jeffrey Stout beyond Relativism," *Journal of Religious Ethics* 24, no. 1 (1996): 125-39.

71. Yoder, *Priestly Kingdom*, 62.

72. Jonathan R. Wilson, *Living Faithfully in a Fragmented World: Lessons for the Church from MacIntyre's After Virtue* (Harrisburg, PA: Trinity Press International, 1997), 24-38.

73. Yoder, "Meaning after Babble," 132; Yoder, *For the Nations*, 61-63.

74. Murphy and Kallenberg, "Anglo-American Postmodernity," 39.

75. Stanley Hauerwas, "The Christian Difference: Or Surviving Postmodernism," in *Anabaptists and Postmodernity*, ed. Susan Biesecker-Mast and Gerald Biesecker-Mast (Telford, PA: Pandora Press U.S., 2000), 50.

Chapter 4

John Howard Yoder and the Politics of Creation

Branson Parler

John Howard Yoder's critique of Reformed theology starts at the very beginning, with Genesis 1–2.[1] Yoder is particularly suspicious of certain Reformed views of the cultural mandate, sphere sovereignty, the concept of vocation, and the doctrine of "creation orders"—all of which originate with interpretations of this text. While Yoder critiques these points of emphasis, he does not spend much time explicating his own doctrine of creation. The opposite could be said of neo-Calvinism, the strand of Reformed thought on which I will focus in this essay.[2] For many North American heirs of Abraham Kuyper, the doctrine of creation serves as the foundation for philosophy and theology, as well as its understanding of culture, society, history, and vocation. These varied areas are all seen as having roots in Genesis 1–2, especially the cultural mandate of 1:26-28. The identification of humanity as the *imago Dei* also plays an important role for many neo-Calvinist thinkers.[3] If one were to traffic in theological stereotypes, one might say that the neo-Calvinist tradition focuses on humanity's place in creation to the neglect of Christ, whereas Yoder focuses on the normativity of Jesus Christ without bothering to relate that normativity to Genesis 1–2 and the *imago Dei*.[4]

This essay seeks to further Anabaptist-Reformed dialogue by arguing that Yoder does indeed have a doctrine of creation, though not very explicit, and by making a few suggestions regarding *what* is entailed in his view.[5] This presents possibilities for convergence between his thought and the neo-Calvinist tradition, while continuing to recognize that real differences remain. To outline Yoder's thought on creation, I will first examine his critique of how creation has functioned in Christian theology and social ethics and then articulate a constructive Yoderian doctrine of creation, drawing upon his doctrine of the Powers. In doing so, I will argue that Yoder gives us several clues that indicate that the redemption accomplished in Jesus is not only a "new creation" (discontinuity) but also a restoration or renewal of creation (continuity). After laying this groundwork, I will conclude by discussing implications for Anabaptist-Reformed dialogue, specifically as the doctrine of creation relates to culture and the nature of the state.[6]

Yoder's Critique of Creation as a Source for Theology and Ethics

In chapter 1 of *The Politics of Jesus,* Yoder sets forth his question for the book and perhaps his whole theology: What are the sources from which the church draws in order to articulate social, political, and ethical norms?[7] Yoder gives a variety of ways this question is answered by what he calls "mainstream Christian ethics." Despite the variety in answers, Yoder sees commonality in that they all "set the authority of Jesus aside, not by avowing that one chooses not to follow him, nor by reading the story and finding in it a different message, but by claiming that in one way or another Jesus' claims on the disciple's life are set aside a priori, on systematic logical grounds."[8] Consequently, they look elsewhere than Jesus for guidance. Yoder states, "all of them thus find in this other *channel* of ethical insight also another *substance* of ethical instruction," a substance that is a "competitive revelation claim."[9] He gives four critiques regarding these "other sources"; I will focus specifically on creation as another source.[10] In addition to illuminating Yoder's views, this will point toward a doctrine of creation that would allow convergence between Yoder's thought and the neo-Calvinist tradition.

The first critique Yoder offers is that creation is considered "self-evident."[11] This is a problem because the notion of self-evidence, taken on its own, is too plastic, and thus able to be used and abused by almost any ethic.[12] Furthermore, a self-evident approach to creation risks downplaying the structural effects of the fall and the epistemological effects of human sin. So Yoder states, "Of course we have access to the good creation of God. What we do not have is epistemologically reliable access which would permit us by looking at the fallen order or analyzing our words about it to know just what is the created goodness and how to disentangle it from the perversion and rebelliousness."[13] Consequently, reference to creation must entail a keen awareness of sin and its effects. This is one point where Yoder understands his views to be different from what he considers to be the Calvinist position:

> Contrasted to the Calvinist vision, then, [my] view is more serious about the fallenness of the structures of creation. For Calvinism, the fall is affirmed but it is held not to mar the orders so seriously as to keep them from being reliably known and moderately made usable to provide a reasonable frame for humane existence. This fallenness is structural: they are warped. It is functional: they do not do their duty. It is noetic: we are not able to perceive by looking at things as they are what they really should be.[14]

The fact of human sin therefore disturbs any appeals to the "self-evident" creation.[15]

Yoder secondly sees ethics that draw on creation as inherently conservative, undergirding and legitimating the status quo (one example is apartheid).[16] Since those in positions of civil power, including the early Reformers, have appealed to creation more often than those on the underside of society,[17] creation appears, to Yoder, unable to provide the resources necessary for "guiding and motivating dissent" in an unjust situation.[18] Thus, when put to use by conservat*ism*, creation becomes a code word for the ungodly dominance of one group over another.[19]

Yoder's third concern is that creation is thought to ground ethics that are more general than the particular ethics one finds in Jesus. This move has two deleterious aspects. First, it conflates church and world by forgetting the difference that faith makes for moral behavior. Second, this search for a general or universal ethics often implies a Constantinian epistemology or hard foundationalism.[20] According to Yoder, a Constantinian epistemology is driven by the desire, not just to be true, but to be irresistible.[21] Deep down, this position is more concerned with legitimating its desire to run society than with being faithful disciples of Jesus.

The fourth and most significant of Yoder's critiques of creation is that it is ascribed content that is not complementary or even supplementary to Jesus but is *opposed* to the normative revelation of Jesus.[22] Yoder is not against creation as such; he is against construing creation as contradictory to what is revealed in Jesus. This is seen in his comments on Romans 2:14:

> Paul doesn't say that people know by nature a law which is different from what we know by revelation. He says they know by nature the same law we know by revelation. Gentiles know naturally that they should do the same works that we know from Moses that we should do. So that is formally just the opposite from the function of the theology of nature when it calls for action different from the commands of Jesus. So if you can use that passage of Paul to say there is natural knowledge, that some can have apart from Moses or the work of Jesus, you can't use this to say that there is a natural knowledge *against* the teaching of Jesus or of Moses or of the prophets, which is precisely what the doctrine of natural law means.[23]

Yoder has no problem with Christians gleaning social-ethical insight from sources other than the witness of Jesus and even of Scripture.[24] Jesus is Lord of the cosmos, not just of the church. These other sources, however, must be persistently and consistently measured against the normative revelation of God in Christ.

Ultimately, what Yoder desires is coherence between doxology, doctrine, and Christian social ethics—between what the church says it believes and how it lives.[25] Yoder therefore cautions that a focus on creation may unwittingly dodge the core confession of Christianity: the full humanity and divinity of Jesus Christ. As Yoder cogently asks, "What becomes of the meaning of the incarnation if Jesus is not normatively human? If he is human but not normative, is this not the ancient ebionitic heresy? If he be somehow authoritative, but not in his humanness, is this not a new gnosticism?"[26] Hence, Yoder states that he is simply trying to take Nicea and Chalcedon seriously.[27] In other words, whatever we say about humanity's true purpose and calling in creation, we cannot disconnect it from the biblical proclamation that Jesus is the true image of God and the Word by whom all things were created. As a result, whatever revelation, substantive doctrine, and ethical guidance we find in creation, these must not be articulated in conflict with the fullness of revelation that is given in Jesus Christ.

While Yoder rejects certain construals and abuses of an appeal to creation, I have shown that his objections do not preclude looking to creation as a source of and for theology and social ethics. As Yoder himself states, "If truly, as John says, the Word without which nothing was made that was made became flesh and tented among us in the man Jesus, then no a priori dichotomy between creation and gospel can be accepted."[28] Thus it is both possible and worthwhile to pursue the topic of creation in relation to Yoder's work in an attempt to uncover his own view of creation, humanity's place in creation, and how those themes are connected in Jesus Christ.

The Powers and Creation

In the epilogue to the chapter "Christ and the Powers," Yoder claims "it would not be too much to claim that the Pauline cosmology of the powers represents an alternative to the dominant ("Thomist") vision of 'natural law' as a more biblical way systematically to relate Christ and creation."[29] He also later states that "what really needs to be debated is a Christian view of human nature."[30] I would suggest that it is in this discussion of the Powers and the relationship of Christ to the Powers that we uncover Yoder's answer to the Reformed notion of "creation order" or the Catholic doctrine of "natural law," both of which say something about creation in general and humanity's specific role in creation. This section thus intends to answer the question posed by Richard Mouw: "When we live out these patterns of discipleship [the "politics of Jesus"] are we also reestablishing the politics of the original creation?"[31] Mouw goes on to note that Anabaptists do not typically worry about the answer to this question. What I intend to show is that Yoder's thought does indeed answer Mouw's question—in the affirmative.

Three points are worth making about Yoder's view of the Powers, human power, and creation. The first significant characteristic of the Powers, according to Yoder, is their participation in the original good creation,[32] which is characterized by "the reign of order among creatures, order which in its original intention is a divine gift."[33] However, it must also be recognized that the Powers and humanity have become fallen. As a result, "the structures which were supposed to be our *servants* have become our *masters* and our *guardians*."[34] Thus, having turned aspects of the good creation into idols, Yoder states that we cannot live *without* the Powers, as they are integral to creation, and yet, we cannot live *with* them, as they harm and enslave humanity.[35] Yet, it is important to note that creation and the power imbued to humanity in creation, is originally good, not ambivalent. As Yoder declares, "the Powers as such, power in itself, is the good creation of God."[36] The problem is not with the power of or in creation; the problem is that humanity has exercised power, the good gift of God, in ways that are *over*-powering, ways that enslave others for selfish gain, rather than in ways that are *em*powering, ways that lead to mutual flourishing.

How is the problem of sin and the Powers overcome? In redemption, Yoder argues, Jesus has broken the oppressive idolatry of the Powers and is continuing to free humanity through the power of his Spirit. Importantly, because exercising power is constitutive of the human condition, redemption is not a release from a relation to the Powers or power.[37] Instead, the redemption manifest in Jesus is a revelation of the true nature of God-like power, that is, what it means to be the true image of God.[38] Because the Powers were originally meant to serve in the call to love, Jesus refused to let them gain mastery over him and would not sacrifice his neighbor to any power, a refusal seen most clearly in his rejection of holy war against Rome.[39] In sacrificing one's neighbor to a Power, no matter how apparently good, one abandons the call to love, in which all humanity and creation are bound together. Yoder expresses this well:

> In the politics of rebellious mankind, we are ready to sacrifice persons to causes, even to ideas. General labels like "freedom," or "justice," "socialism" or "capitalism," "order" or "humanism" become positive or negative values in their own right, causes to combat for or destroy. The modern word for this is "ideology." The biblical word that fits best is probably "idol."
>
> In the Spirit of God, the jealous God who wants us to serve none other, there is no such disincarnate or ideal value worthy to demand the sacrifice of the concrete personal and communal values of our real neighbor. Those abstractions will remain valuable in the measure in which they help us better serve our neighbors. They become sinful when we are asked to sacrifice our neighbor to them.[40]

Jesus therefore embodies true human power and freedom, not by "fighting fire with fire,"—i.e., combating the Powers with violence, manipulation, and idolatry—but as the second Adam, by living a life of wise rule over the fallen Powers. His life, death, resurrection, and ascension broke the oppressive rule of the Powers and redeemed humanity to once again walk in true power and wisdom. Thankfully, in the work of Christ, the Powers have been exposed as false gods and conquered by the humble rule of Jesus, the representative of true humanity, whose victory results in "an authentic restored humanity."[41]

This language of restoration brings us to a central issue: Yoder's view of the nature of creation. To aid in grasping Yoder's position, it is helpful to keep in mind Thomas Finger's distinction between two views of creation: the "completed creation" and the "open creation."[42] In the former, both the natural and human world are given fixed forms, or at least latent possibilities of development. In this view, the original creation is not just good but perfect, meaning that redemption must be a return to this state. This view could be seen as grace restores nature. The latter view, the "open creation," sees creation as "open for development and pointed toward eschatological perfection."[43] In other words, grace perfects nature. This view emphasizes redemption as a renewal of creation that reopens the movement of creation toward its eschatological goal. Thus, redemption does not simply try to go back to the past but is a movement from and toward the eschatological future.

In Yoder's theology, there is a sense in which Christ both restores creation and perfects creation. This "open" view of creation is operative in Yoder's explanation of Christ's work of "restoring the cosmos."[44] Thus, Yoder states that his interpretation of Scripture "does not seek to take history 'back to Go' but rather enables authentic progress."[45] Hence, the politics of Jesus do not simply restore a static structure or order that existed in the beginning; rather, the dynamic human freedom and power to be in right relation with God and all creation is restored—a restoration so radical that it can only be termed *new creation*. In this renewal, the Powers take their place as servants of humanity, rather than oppressive masters of humanity.[46] The goal of the church, as empowered by the Holy Spirit, is to bear witness to the fact that Christ is Lord and, consequently, the idolatrous power of the Powers has been broken and they are being made the footstool of Christ.

Importantly, however, Christ is not disconnected from humanity's anchoring in creation. Indeed, how could we possibly pit creation order or natural law against Christ, given John 1, Colossians 1, and Hebrews 1?[47] So, as Yoder says, "An ethic of *torah* or *halakah*, or an ethic of discipleship, is therefore deeper, more rooted in the nature of things, than an ethic which seeks to manipulate the causal nexus for the best."[48] Elsewhere

Yoder notes that Jesus' acceptance of the cross is not only an eschatological decision (based on where God is taking creation), but "an ontological decision, dictated by a truer picture of what the world *really* is."[49] The same logic applies to followers of Christ: "the way of discipleship is the way for which we are made; there is no other 'nature' to which grace is a *superadditum*."[50] Yoder summarizes the proper approach to nature and grace, creation and Christ, in this way:

> When society has been defined as the nation and social order as patriarchy, then it is no longer true that grace completes nature; in the face of that definition of "nature," the word of YHWH has to be like a fire, like a hammer that breaks rocks into pieces.
>
> Yet when the "nature of things" is properly defined, the organic relationship to grace is restored. The cross is not a scandal to those who know the world as God sees it, but only to the pagans, who look for what they call wisdom, or the Judeans, who look for what they call power.. This is what I meant before, when I stated that the choice of Jesus was ontological: it risks an option in favor of the restored vision of *how things really are.*[51]

That is why it can be said that cross-bearers work "with the grain of the universe" or that "the shape of the universe is such that to return good for evil is functional."[52] In answer to the question posed by Mouw at the beginning of this section, I have shown that what is revealed, renewed, and restored in the politics of Jesus is the authentic power of creation. Far from detaching redemption from creation, Yoder provides a broad outline of their radical connection in the politics of Jesus and the power of creation, in humanity's true being and calling.

Implications for Anabaptist-Reformed Dialogue

Given that Yoder *does* have a doctrine of creation and that it coheres with the revelation of God in Jesus Christ, how might neo-Calvinism take Yoder's view of creation seriously, such that it impacts the doctrine of creation with specific reference to the theological implications of Genesis 1–2 in general and Genesis 1:26-28 (the cultural mandate) in particular? In this section, I note how attending to Yoder's doctrine of creation may point the way to further convergence between Yoder and the neo-Calvinist tradition in two key areas: culture and politics. Before answering this question, it should be noted that both Yoder and Mouw make clear that Anabaptist-Reformed dialogue is not a "classical dilemma" in the sense that there is a logical contradiction built into the nature of the debate so that one has to take one stance or the other. Rather, the discussion is a dynamic, ongoing, and intra-family one.[53]

Creation, Christ, and culture. As noted earlier, creation functions as a chief source for neo-Calvinism's emphasis on culture and cultural involvement. What are the implications of attending to Yoder's articulation of the connection between Christ and creation? Stated one way, neo-Calvinists should not allow the paradigm of Niebuhr's *Christ and Culture* to frame the nature of the discussion with Anabaptists.[54] Stated more positively, if both parties are attentive to the self-description and historical realities faced by both traditions, we can begin to see where the real issues lie.

With respect to creation, Christ, and culture, the shape of the dialogue should revolve around the question of *how* Christians are to be cultural beings, not *whether* cultural activity as such is a valid realm for participation. As Yoder often asserts, the cultural mandate is neither univocal nor monolithic.[55] Consequently, it should not be assumed that the substance of the cultural mandate is a given. As most contemporary interlocutors (both Reformed and Anabaptist) would affirm, to be human is to be cultural. However, once this has been acknowledged, to debate "cultural involvement" per se becomes profoundly uninteresting, since the question is not *whether* any human or community is involved culturally but *how* we are to be cultural beings. Therefore, it should be made clear that there are contested interpretations as to precisely what is required of humanity by Genesis 1:26-28 and how this should be manifested in a fallen world, in which proper dominion persistently morphs into improper domination.[56] Just as no Reformed thinker would affirm all possible manifestations of culture or the social order, so no Anabaptist would deny "culture" or denounce "the social order" as such. Once this is acknowledged, then the more truly interesting (and ultimately fruitful) dialogue can begin, in which we address concrete issues of money, power, justice, and peacemaking, and seek to articulate how followers of Jesus can and should live as the church, seeking the peace of the cities where we live. In this context, Reformed and Anabaptist thinkers can debate whether one is *misinterpreting* the cultural mandate, but the notion that Anabaptists *reject* the cultural mandate can and should cease.[57]

Furthermore, given the goodness of creation and the corruption brought by the fall, it should be recognized that the Christian and the church do not necessarily take the same stance toward every segment of culture or cultural artifact. Depending on one's specific location in time, place, and social situation, and depending on historical contingency and cultural variety, it is impossible to assert that we must choose one Niebuhrian mode of interaction (against culture, of culture, transforming culture, etc.) with culture as such.[58] For example, one cannot cite the goodness of God's creation to validate involvement in all economic practices within the current North American context. Some specific practices and possibly entire institutions are unjust and corrupt and therefore should be rejected by Christians. As the dialogue between Reformed and Anabaptist folk continue, both traditions should be attempting to discern what forms of existing North American culture(s) require a stance of conscientious objection and what forms call for conscientious participation.

Creation, the state, and the sword. If Yoder is correct to see Jesus as presenting us with normative human nature, and that this is a revelation of our original calling in creation, then what can we say about the state and its sword-wielding? Is the reality of the state grounded in creation or fall? Many times, the presumptive neo-Calvinist answer is creation.[59] But the views of Kuyper, the Dutch statesman and theologian, are more complex, and it is intriguing to notice some general points of agreement between Yoder and Kuyper.

Kuyper contends that "without sin there would have been neither magistrate nor state-order" and that every formation of the state is in some sense "unnatural."[60] This fact means that there is ambiguity at the heart of the reality of the state and its use of coercive force. On the one hand, the state is a blessing, because it keeps absolute chaos from reigning in human society; on the other hand, it is a curse, since the authority exercised is that of sinful humans, and therefore subject "to all manner of despotic ambitions."[61] Because of this, the state is classified neither under creation nor redemption. Rather, Kuyper asserts that we should gratefully accept its reality as a "means of preservation."[62] The state does not provide the ultimate telos for human life but merely assists in preserving human life and society in a post-lapsarian world so God may continue working to bring creation to its ultimate telos. Importantly, Kuyper seems to be here working with the *prima facie* meaning of the Belgic Confession, Article 36, which states that "We believe that *because of the depravity of the human race* our good God has ordained kings, princes, and civil officers."[63]

Notably, this same point is made by Yoder. In *Christian Witness to the State*, he argues that the sword is a post-lapsarian institution.[64] Yoder elsewhere contends that there is a limited place for the state in the preservation of the fallen cosmos.[65] This does not mean that all states by nature do God's revealed will, but that they are simply "lined up, used by God in the order of the cosmos."[66] This is not a creational order, but a "relative order" instituted because of sin.[67] Consequently, despite (and because of) human sin, there is a limited place for the sword. In a fallen world, Yoder asserts that the state falls under the "order of providence" or preservation, which enables God to use it for his specific purposes. By placing it in the category of preservation, however, Yoder argues that at least the sword, and most likely the state as well, are neither grounded in creation nor involved in bringing about redemption.[68]

Though Kuyper and Yoder both place the state in the category of preservation, they have widely different views of what that means for the Christian. For Kuyper, the office of prime minister of the Netherlands is a worthy pursuit; Yoder sees the Christian holding political office as analogous to the first violinist doing the job of the usher—only the church can be the church, whereas the non-Christian is capable of occupying political office.[69] *The practical payoff, however, of their common view of the nature of the state should issue in many concrete similarities between the Yoderian and Kuyperian.* Since Kuyper affirms that the state is instituted by God, but only on account of human sin, there is an ambiguity at the root of the nature of the state.

Because of this fundamental ambiguity, Christians must be aware of the demonic shape the state can take and carefully discern when and how to be involved in certain state functions. When Christians do become involved in the state, there should be practical structures of accountability in order to ensure faithfulness in the midst of the perennial temptation to misuse one's position of power. Moreover, the church must cultivate awareness that any participation is provisional, so that if holding a position requires the Christian to do something immoral (e.g. fight an unjust war), the Christian will recognize his or her responsibility to give up that position. Without this kind of accountability within the Christian community, the Anabaptist may justly inquire how the neo-Calvinist avoids expanding a limited justification for involvement in the state into wholesale Constantinianism.

The practical implications of Yoder's position are similar. Yoder affirms that the question should not be asked in the abstract (should Christians participate in government?) but in particular (what specific aspects of this government can Christians participate in while remaining faithful followers of Christ?). While he rejects use of the sword, Yoder does not simply write off participation in all aspects of the state. Rather, he calls for the need to persistently evaluate the claims made on human life and behavior by the state and how that may or may not comport with our calling to be witnesses to Jesus Christ.[70] Consequently, the necessary condition for any participation in the state is the existence of a faithful and discerning (not perfect) church, which consistently tests its own life for conformity to Christ.[71]

Like Yoder, there are those within the neo-Calvinist tradition who are clear that, within the political realm, the option is not *either* withdrawal *or* engagement (with the Reformed on one side and the Anabaptist on the other), but *both* selective withdrawal *and* selective engagement.[72] How should Christians make this judgment? Mouw helpfully summarizes:

> Whatever normative status we might still attribute to the data of the political deliverances that were received in the ancient wilderness, and the even more ancient Garden, they are far outweighed by the political ministry of the incarnate Servant Ruler. Let me put my point here as clearly as I can: if there is a seeming tension between the older political advice and the kind of political guidance we receive from Jesus—if, for example, the older way seems to encourage us to use the sword in a manner that the Gospels seem to forbid—then the way of wisdom is to follow what we take to be the Gospel way.[73]

Conclusion

I have argued that although Yoder critiques the way creation often functions in theology and social ethics, he himself does have an incipient doctrine of creation, which I have articulated based upon his view of Christ and the Powers. Given the reality of sin, however, Yoder will not allow for creation to function independently of the revelation of Christ. This, however, does not preclude a doctrine of creation that (like creation itself) coheres with and in Christ. Establishing Yoder's doctrine of creation helps to further the dialogue between Yoder's Anabaptist standpoint and that of the neo-Calvinist tradition, with its strong emphasis on creation. I have shown that clarifying Yoder's own stance enables further insights surrounding the issue of culture and involvement in politics, two often contentious points of disagreement between these traditions. In the end, both are joined by their continued mutual concern to live out the Lordship of Christ in everyday life. Insofar as this is done, walking in the way of wisdom, which may appear as foolishness to the world, both Anabaptist and Reformed will bear witness to the crucified Lamb, who claims every square inch of creation as his proper domain.[74]

Notes

1. For example, see Yoder, "Reformed Versus Anabaptist Social Strategies: An Inadequate Typology," *TSF Bulletin*, May/June 1985, 2-7.

2. By neo-Calvinism, I refer generally to the movement beginning with Abraham Kuyper (1837–1920). Kuyper's 1898 Stone Lectures, *Lectures on Calvinism* (Grand Rapids, MI: Eerdmans, 1961), provide one entry point to his thought. Key figures in Dutch neo-Calvinism include Herman Bavinck (1854–1921), Herman Dooyeweerd (1894–1977), and D. H. Th. Vollenhoven (1892–1978). Like any tradition, neo-Calvinism is not monolithic. For a historical overview of North American neo-Calvinism and key figures therein, see James Bratt, *Dutch Calvinism in America: A History of a Conservative Subculture* (Grand Rapids, MI: Eerdmans, 1984) and John Bolt, "From Princeton to Wheaton: The Course of neo-Calvinism in North America," *Calvin Theological Journal* 42, no. 1 (2007): 65-89. A good introduction to neo-Calvinist thought is Brian J. Walsh and J. Richard Middleton's *The Transforming Vision* (Downer's Grove, IL: InterVarsity Press, 1984) and Albert M. Wolter's *Creation Regained: Biblical Basics for a Reformational Worldview* (Grand Rapids, MI: Eerdmans, 1985).

3. For example, see Herman Dooyeweerd, *Roots of Western Culture: Pagan, Secular, and Christian Options*, trans. John Kraay, ed. Mark Vander Vennen and Bernard Zylstra (Toronto: Wedge Publishing Foundation, 1979), 64; and Walsh and Middleton, *The Transforming Vision*, 52-59.

4. As Calvin Redekop notes, creation is generally not attended to in the historic Anabaptist confessions of faith. "Toward a Mennonite Theology and Ethic of Creation," *Mennonite Quarterly Review* 60, no. 3 (1986): 387-403, esp. 394, n27.

5. On Anabaptist-Reformed dialogue, see Richard J. Mouw, "Abandoning the Typology: A Reformed Assist," *TSF Bulletin*, May/June 1985, 7-10. Yoder and Mouw later collaborated on "Evangelical Ethics and the Anabaptist-Reformed Dialogue," *The Journal of Religious Ethics* 17, no. 2

(1989): 121-37. Mouw provides further elaboration in "Creational Politics: Some Calvinist Amendments," *Christian Scholar's Review* 23, no. 2 (1993): 181-93. Yoder's doctoral work focused on the dialogues between the Swiss Anabaptists and Reformers from 1523–1538. Yoder, *Anabaptism and Reformation in Switzerland: A Historical and Theological Analysis of the Dialogues Between the Anabaptists and Reformers*, trans. David Carl Stassen and C. Arnold Snyder, ed. C. Arnold Snyder (Kitchener, ON: Pandora, 2004).

6. It should be recognized that we could say "political authority" rather than "state," since the modern nation-state is one particular way political authority can be configured. Since Yoder often refers to the state, I will follow that usage in this essay as well.

7. Yoder, *The Politics of Jesus*, 2nd ed. (Grand Rapids, MI: Eerdmans, 1994) 4-8.

8. Ibid., 20. Cf. Yoder, "Why Ecclesiology is Social Ethics," in *The Royal Priesthood: Essays Ecclesiological and Ecumenical*, ed. Michael G. Cartwright (Grand Rapids, MI: Eerdmans, 1994), 114.

9. Yoder, "Christ, the Light of the World," in *The Royal Priesthood*, 189.

10. The term "creation" can be broad and vague. It could mean (1) the biophysical world, (2) theological anthropology rooted in the fact that humans are creatures made in God's image, (3) the first act in the biblical narrative, (4) the creation order/natural law, and (5) the realm of culture—using God's gifts imparted in nature and human nature. I will not attempt to strictly define the term, but leave it open to this range of interrelated meaning.

11. Yoder, *Politics of Jesus*, 19.

12. Yoder, *The Christian Witness to the State* (Newton, KS: Faith and Life Press, 1964), 33.

13. Yoder, "Behold, My Servant Shall Prosper," in *Karl Barth and the Problem of War and Other Essays on Barth*, ed. Mark Thiessen Nation (Eugene, OR: Cascade Books), 163.

14. Ibid.

15. Yoder, "Sacrament as Social Process: Christ the Transformer of Culture," in *The Royal Priesthood*, 370.

16. Yoder, "Creation and Gospel," *Perspectives: A Journal of Reformed Thought* 3, no. 8 (Oct. 1988): 8-10. See also "The Hermeneutics of Peoplehood," in *The Priestly Kingdom: Social Ethics as Gospel* (Notre Dame, IN: University of Notre Dame Press, 1984), 40. Middleton helps negotiate the difficulties surrounding creation theology and conservatism in "Is Creation Theology Inherently Conservative? A Dialogue with Walter Brueggemann," *Harvard Theological Review* 87, no. 3 (1994): 257-77. Although addressing Brueggemann's work, much of Middleton's insight could be applied to Yoder.

17. Yoder, *Body Politics: Five Practices of the Christian Community*

Before the Watching World (Scottdale, PA: Herald Press, 2001), 26. For comments on conservatism and a similar critique of the neo-Calvinist tradition from within, see Nicholas Wolterstorff, *Until Justice and Peace Embrace* (Grand Rapids, MI: Eerdmans, 1983), 59.

18. Yoder, *Politics of Jesus*, 19.

19. An example would be South Africa. See John W. de Gruchy, *The Church Struggle in South Africa* (Grand Rapids, MI: Eerdmans, 1979), 202.

20. Yoder, "The Hermeneutics of Peoplehood," in *The Priestly Kingdom*, 42. Cf. Yoder, "On Not Being Ashamed of the Gospel: Particularity, Pluralism, and Validation," *Faith and Philosophy* 9, no. 3 (1992): 286, and "Walk and Word," in *Theology Without Foundations: Religious Practice and the Future of Theological Truth*, ed. Stanley Hauerwas, Nancey Murphy, and Mark Nation (Nashville: Abingdon Press, 1994), 77-90. Chris K. Huebner refers to Yoder's position as a "pacifist epistemology" in "Globalization, Theory, and Dialogical Vulnerability: John Howard Yoder and the Possibility of a Pacifist Epistemology," *Mennonite Quarterly Review* 76, no. 1 (2002): 49-62. See also Ted Grimsrud, "Pacifism and Knowing: 'Truth' in the Theological Ethics of John Howard Yoder," *Mennonite Quarterly Review* 77, no. 3 (2003): 403-16.

21. Yoder, "On Not Being Ashamed," 287.

22. Yoder, "Sacrament as Social Process," in *The Royal Priesthood*, 370.

23. Yoder, *Christian Attitudes Toward War, Peace, and Revolution: A Companion to Bainton* (Elkhart, IN: Co-op Bookstore, 1983), 48.

24. Yoder, "Radical Reformation Ethics," in *The Priestly Kingdom*, 120.

25. This is one of Craig A. Carter's central theses in *The Politics of the Cross: The Theology and Social Ethics of John Howard Yoder* (Grand Rapids, MI: Brazos, 2001), 17.

26. Yoder, *Politics of Jesus*, 10.

27. Ibid., 102.

28. Yoder, "Creation and Gospel," 8.

29. Ibid., 159.

30. Yoder, *Politics of Jesus*, 240.

31. Mouw, "Creational Politics," 191.

32. Yoder, *Politics of Jesus*, 143.

33. Ibid., 141.

34. Ibid. (emphasis added).

35. Ibid., 143.

36. Ibid., 154.

37. Ibid., 138.

38. See J. Richard Middleton, *The Liberating Image: The Imago Dei in Genesis 1–2* (Grand Rapids, MI: Brazos, 2005), for a study of the *imago Dei* that is consonant with Yoder's notion of power and Jesus as the true image of God.

39. Yoder, *Politics of Jesus*, 141.

40. Yoder, "The Spirit of God and the Politics of Men," in *For the Nations: Essays Public and Evangelical* (Grand Rapids, MI: Eerdmans, 1997), 232.

41. Yoder, *Politics of Jesus*, 145.

42. Thomas Finger, *Systematic Theology: An Eschatological Approach*, Vol. 2 (Scottdale, PA: Herald Press, 1985), 412-13.

43. Ibid., 413.

44. Yoder, "Are You the One Who is to Come?" in *For the Nations*, 214.

45. Yoder, "The Power Equation, Jesus, and the Politics of King," in *For the Nations*, 140, n29.

46. Cf. Hendrik Berkhof, *Christ and the Powers*, trans. John Howard Yoder (Scottdale, PA: Herald Press, 1962), 49.

47. See Yoder, "'But We Do See Jesus'," in *The Priestly Kingdom*, 49-54.

48. Yoder, "Ethics and Eschatology," *Ex Auditu* 6 (1990): 126.

49. Yoder, "Are You the One Who Is to Come?" in *For the Nations*, 211.

50. Yoder, "The Hermeneutics of Peoplehood," in *The Priestly Kingdom*, 36. Cf. Herman Bavinck, *Reformed Dogmatics, Vol. 2: God and Creation*, trans. John Vriend, ed. John Bolt, (Grand Rapids, MI: Baker, 2004), 551.

51. Yoder, "Are You the One Who Is to Come?" in *For the Nations*, 212 (emphasis added).

52. Yoder, "Armaments and Eschatology," *Studies in Christian Ethics* 1, no. 1 (1988): 58, and "The Power Equation, Jesus, and the Politics of King," in *For the Nations*, 147. Cf. Stanley Hauerwas, *With the Grain of the Universe* (Grand Rapids, MI: Baker, 2001), 218-25.

53. Yoder and Mouw, "Anabaptist-Reformed Dialogue," 127-29.

54. For critical readings of how H. R. Niebuhr has both hindered and helped the discussion, see Glen H. Stassen, D. M. Yeager, and Yoder, ed., *Authentic Transformation: A New Vision of Christ and Culture* (Nashville: Abingdon, 1996) and Craig A Carter, *Rethinking Christ and Culture: A Post-Christendom Perspective* (Grand Rapids, MI: Brazos, 2006).

55. For example, see Yoder, "A Critique of Christ and Culture," 54-57, and "Reformed versus Anabaptist Social Strategies," 5.

56. Yoder, "Reformed Versus Anabaptist Social Strategies," 5.

57. Cf. Duane K. Friesen's *Artists, Citizens, Philosophers Seeking the Peace of the City: An Anabaptist Theology of Culture* (Scottdale, PA: Herald Press, 2000).

58. For example, see Yoder, "Critique of *Christ and Culture*," 54-57.

59. E.g., Walsh and Middleton, *The Transforming Vision*, 55, mention "political life" as grounded in creation; Wolters, *Creation Regained*, 22, states that "the civil authority belongs to the created order; the state is founded in an ordinance of God."

60. Kuyper, *Lectures*, 81. For a nuanced discussion of this point, see Mouw, *Politics and the Biblical Drama* (Grand Rapids, MI: Baker, 1976), 32-36.

61. Kuyper, *Lectures*, 81.

62. Kuyper, *Lectures*, 82.

63. English text in *Ecumenical Creeds and Reformed Confessions* (Grand Rapids, MI: CRC Publications, 1988), (emphasis added).

64. Yoder, *Christian Witness*, 34.

65. Ibid., 36.

66. Yoder, *Politics of Jesus*, 202.

67. Yoder, *Discipleship as Political Responsibility*, trans. Timothy J. Geddert (Scottdale, PA: Herald Press, 2003), 18-19.

68. Yoder, "Behold My Servant Shall Prosper," 163.

69. Yoder, *Politics of Jesus*, 198. Cf. *Discipleship as Political Responsibility*, 45.

70. Yoder, *Discipleship as Political Responsibility*, 40-41.

71. Yoder, "Civil Religion in America," in *The Priestly Kingdom*, 188-89.

72. For example, see H. Evan Runner, *Scriptural Religion and Political Task* (Toronto: Wedge, 1974); Mouw, "Providence and Politics," in *Life is Religion: Essays in Honor of H. Evan Runner*, ed. Henry Vander Goot (St. Catharines, ON: Paideia Press, 1981); and Brian J. Walsh and Sylvia Keesmaat, *Colossians Remixed* (Downer's Grove, IL: InterVarsity Press, 2004): 147-68.

73. Mouw, "Creational Politics," 193. Mouw goes on to note that he has not concluded with finality that the "if" clauses are entirely correct, but that they must ever remain at the forefront of Anabaptist-Reformed dialogue.

74. Thanks to John Nugent, Nicholas Ansell, and Craig A. Carter for their insightful comments and suggestions on portions or the entirety of this essay.

Chapter 5

Freedom of the Cross:
John Howard Yoder and Womanist Theologies in Conversation

Nekeisha Alexis-Baker

For many Christians, the blood of Jesus is the means by which salvation is secured. For many Black Christians in particular, the power of Jesus' blood sustains them through the daily injustices they face in racialized American society and is a sign of Jesus' promise to care for them in times of need and struggle. But does a theology that glorifies and centralizes Jesus' suffering and violent death also disempower and thwart the survival of people who are oppressed?

Being a Black Mennonite woman I approach this question from at least two perspectives. As a Mennonite, I am part of a tradition that is inspired by sixteenth-century Anabaptist martyrs and emphasizes following Jesus' countercultural teachings and example—even in the face of hostility. As a Black woman, I am also drawn to the womanist task of addressing "the spiritual, ecclesial, social, political and economic implications of the 'tri-dimensional phenomenon of race, class and gender oppression' in the experience of African-American women."[1] Yet womanist theologians assert that Jesus' cross, while accepted as redemptive throughout Christian tradition, can reinforce Black women's subjugation. In an attempt to hold these two viewpoints together, I have sought to facilitate a conversation between womanist theology and John Howard Yoder's thought, which has influenced Mennonite theology and practice throughout the twentieth century and has been instrumental in my faith formation. In so doing, I have discovered that these seemingly contradictory perspectives support one another in liberating Black people and freeing the cross from being used as an instrument of oppression.

The Cross in Black Subjugation

During slavery in America, Black people encountered a Christian faith that justified their oppression. White Christians evangelized slaves with sermons, catechetical programs, and proof-texts that spiritualized the freedom and equality available in Christ,[2] and sanctioned the traffic and abuse of African people.[3] Masters and missionaries alike supported slavery with a "hermeneutics of sacrifice" that glorified "personal sacrifice in the imitation of Christ as the *sine qua non* of Christian character."[4] Rooted in the early church's high regard for martyrdom and in an understanding of Jesus as the atoning sacrifice who dies in our place, this theology exhorted slaves and other subordinate groups to see their oppression as "service owed to God."[5]

In spite of these messages, Black people adopted and adapted Jesus' cross in ways that enabled them to survive their enslavement. They saw Jesus' suffering as a sign of his solidarity with them, conflated his suffering with their own,[6] and contextualized their oppression within a Christian framework. For some slaves, Jesus' victory over death in the resurrection inspired them to struggle for their freedom.[7] Others developed a sacramental understanding of their suffering in which they, like Jesus, demonstrated God's love to the world. This belief gave them "moral agency . . . to worship God and love others" in spite of the violence inflicted upon them.[8] While relating their suffering to the cross in these ways empowered many slaves, other ways of explaining their situation only reinforced their oppression. Some slaves saw their bondage as divine punishment for being heathens and as God's way of converting them to Christianity. Still others concluded that "it was Christian to be victimized and to be requited in the end,"[9] just as Jesus was undeservedly killed on the cross and resurrected. Although these and other ways of understanding Jesus' crucifixion helped slaves make sense of their suffering, womanists argue that it is detrimental for Black women to identify with a savior whose innocent suffering at the hands of, in place of, and for the redemption of a hostile world is perceived to be sacred.

In *Sisters in the Wilderness*, Delores Williams discusses Black women's history of surrogacy and questions whether a surrogate-God figure has saving power for us.[10] During slavery, Black women experienced coerced surrogacy in which dominant people and institutions forced them to assume roles that would usually be filled by White men and women, and Black men. As mammies, Black women nursed and nurtured White children in place of their White mothers. As breeders, they were forced to produce children to whom they had no claim. As sexual objects, Black women were violated to fulfill White and Black men's sexual appetites. As house slaves, they were occasionally forced to manage the plantation in their slave-owners' absences.[11]

Black women's surrogacy continued into the postbellum period. Although they were no longer slaves, social and economic pressures compelled them to accept work as domestic servants, taking care of White women's children and homes, and to assume the traditional head-of-household role in the absence of Black men.[12] Black women's surrogacy extends even into the present. With Black men being incarcerated at least 9.6 times the rate of White men and one in every twenty Black man over the age of eighteen in state or federal prison,[13] many Black women continue to serve as mothers and fathers to their children, and as their family's main economic provider. In addition, African-American, African, and Caribbean women still serve as domestic help in White households. Women who serve in these roles without legal immigration status or economic security often work as many as eighty hours per week without employment benefits and are often verbally and physically abused.[14]

Black women also experience the hermeneutics of sacrifice within the Black community. For example, during the Civil Rights Movement, many Black women believed that opposing sexism within the Black community distracted from efforts to resist racism, neglecting their need for gender equality in the process.[15] Such self-sacrifice persists today as members of the Black community at large and Black churches in particular romanticize or deny Black women's suffering. This occurs when Black women who are physically, sexually, and emotionally abused are pressured to remain silent or encouraged to "bear [their] cross in faith."[16] It is also prevalent when Black women are praised for being pillars of support and simultaneously denounced "as the root cause of the demise of the Black community."[17] These and numerous other injustices committed against Black women are frequently bolstered by a christology that valorizes suffering.

Randall Kenan's short story, "The Strange and Tragic Ballad of Mabel Pearsall" illustrates how this principle of sacrifice can function in Black women's daily lives. In this work of fiction, Mabel is under emotional assault by disrespectful students, a patronizing White male principal, an insensitive and detached husband, and two children who take advantage of her. Over time, her good Christian façade weakens as she serves on too many committees, deals with too many unanswered prayers, and feels humiliated by a young, single mother who threatens her marriage. As her anxiety increases, Mabel is comforted by seeing herself as "a good and faithful servant" who is "Washed in the Blood of the Lamb."[18] As Mabel increasingly sacrifices her personal, professional and spiritual life, the cross that helps her cope also sanctions her oppression, which leads to her undoing.

The Cross in Womanist Theology

In light of this history of subjugation, Williams questions the redemptive power of Jesus' cross for Black women. In her view, "The image of Jesus on the cross is the image of human sin in its most desecrated form"[19] and for this reason, the cross should not be glorified. By naming the cross as "defilement"[20] Williams hopes to liberate Black women from the false belief that God ordains their surrogate roles. Instead of focusing on the cross, she concentrates on Jesus' life and "ministerial vision"—his raising the dead, healing the sick, exorcising evil, righting relationships and ministry of compassion and love—and identifies these as salvific.[21] Another womanist approach to the cross is to emphasize Jesus' resurrection as the source of salvation. For example, Jacquelyn Grant sees the resurrection as a promise to Black women that their exploitation is not permanent: it "signifies that their tri-dimensional oppressive existence is not the end, but it merely represents the context in which a particular people struggle to experience hope and liberation."[22] For some womanists, Jesus' life and resurrection become the primary signs of triumph over evil.

In their emphasis on the life and resurrection of Jesus, womanists challenge Christian traditions that spiritualize and make irrelevant the words and work of Christ. Instead of seeing the cross as a divine act to be glorified, they name his suffering on the cross as a result of human sin and of Jesus' confrontation with that sin. Yet even as womanists attempt to decentralize the cross in Christian faith, it remains essential to Jesus' story and to Black spirituality. Jesus' crucifixion is still a focal point in Black preaching and teaching and an indispensable symbol that unifies this community in its struggle for freedom and equality.[23] As a result, "these symbols and their accompanying meanings will not be easily disregarded in the Christian tradition in general or the Black Christian tradition in particular."[24] In response to this reality, Christians would do well to craft theologies of atonement that enable Black women and others plagued by injustice to experience the freedom that is already available in Jesus. John Howard Yoder's theology of the cross supports this reinterpreting endeavor, even as it raises important questions for and is critiqued by womanism.

Freeing the Cross for Liberation

In *The Politics of Jesus*, Yoder writes, "The cross of Christ was not an inexplicable or chance event, which happened to strike him, like illness or accident. . . . The cross of Calvary was not a difficult family situation, not a frustration of visions of personal fulfillment, a crushing debt or a nagging in-law."[25] In *For the Nations: Essays Evangelical and Public*, he similarly critiques David Garrow for identifying Martin Luther King Jr.'s battles with depression, sexual misconduct, and self-doubt as parts of the cross he bore. Although these struggles are significant, Yoder insists that they not be likened to Jesus' crucifixion,[26] which was the "political, legally-to-be-expected result of a moral clash with the powers of his ruling society."[27] For Yoder:

> The believer's cross is no longer any and every kind of suffering, sickness or tension, the bearing of which is demanded. The believer's cross is, like that of Jesus, the price of social nonconformity. It is not, like sickness or catastrophe, an inexplicable, unpredictable suffering; it is the end of a path freely chosen after counting the cost. . . . It is the social reality of representing in an unwilling world the Order to come.[28]

Critical to this understanding is Yoder's belief that the cross stands in contrast to the crown that dominates, to violent revolution *and* to being the quiet in the land.[29] It is the result of Jesus' voluntary decision to reject violence, hate, hostility, and non-involvement in confronting the powers. Subsequently, when one takes up the cross and follows Christ, one makes a conscious choice to vulnerably resist injustice and renounces the paths of premature peace and violent insurrection.[30]

By naming what the cross is not, Yoder subverts the hermeneutics of sacrifice that sanctifies Black women's pain and encourages resistance to oppression as a way to follow Jesus. Yoder's theology of the cross also undercuts religious rationales for Black people's subjugation precisely because the suffering they experience is not a valid "way of the cross." By identifying the particular kind of suffering that is manifest in Jesus' cross, his theology supports womanist work to liberate Black women from viewing our violated bodies, surrogacy, and oppression as our crosses to bear. Furthermore, Yoder's emphasis on the voluntary nature of the cross enables Christians to thoroughly denounce any and all abuses that are imposed upon Black women and other underprivileged groups. When the church understands that Jesus' cross is the response of a hostile world to his freely chosen path of nonviolence, identification with the poor, justice and reconciliation, it is better able to expose, critique, and confront suffering that does not fit Jesus' example—whether its racial discrimination, domestic violence, sexual abuse or emotional neglect.

Although Yoder's theology of the cross is liberating for Black women it also calls into question some womanists' use of cross language. For example, JoAnne Marie Terrell describes picking cotton as a child saying, "the sight of black bodies, en masse, picking cotton on white-owned plantations was to my imaginative and already theologically oriented mind a facsimile of Jesus' crucifixion."[31] Douglas makes a similar observation, writing, "The suffering of slavery and the suffering of the cross were synonymous."[32] Williams extends the metaphor even further, equating cross-bearing with being a single parent, living on welfare, having inadequate healthcare, and being victimized by domestic violence, sexism, and racism.[33] Similarly, Grant describes the "abuses, physical and verbal, the dehumanization, the pains, the sufferings, the loss of families and friends and the disruption of communities" facing Black people as "cross experiences."[34] However, if we accept Yoder's view that the cross is the world's response to a conscious decision to live out Jesus' ethic—if we concur that the cross is a "political punishment"[35]—then womanists can also be challenged for conflating these types of suffering with Jesus' crucifixion.

Womanists would likely respond to this critique by identifying similarities between Black people's oppression and Jesus' political execution. Like Jesus, Black people have been abused at the hands of a racist system that has included discriminatory laws and government policies, and state-sponsored violence. Like the Jewish Jesus, Black people share a low status in society and their persecution has been undeserved. Like Jesus, Black people hung from trees for "getting out of line," liberating others and simply being who we are. Since Black people's oppression is indeed "sociopsychological, psychocultural, economic and political,"[36] womanists might argue that it is fitting to characterize the injustices experienced by Black people and by Black women in particular as the cross of Christ.

Although I concur that Black people's suffering is political and sympathize with womanist uses of cross-language, I nevertheless believe that it is important to adopt other images to describe our plight precisely because the cross is still widely glorified in the church. In my view, equating the rape of Black women during slavery with Jesus' crucifixion as Grant does[37] while many Christians continue to valorize Rome's harrowing violence against Jesus risks supporting theologies of the cross that already undercut Black women. Therefore, womanists can only further their liberating work by seeking alternative images for Black women's oppression. Perhaps if we used analogies that did not easily substitute Black women's subjugation with Jesus' crucifixion, it would do even more to prohibit sexist pastors, racist church leaders and even women like Mabel from justifying and sanctifying Black women's pain.

Freeing the Cross for Transformation

In addition to naming what the cross is not, Yoder also includes the concept of revolutionary subordination in his theology of the cross. Derived from his reading of Ephesians 5:21–6:9 and Colossians 3:18–4:1, Yoder sees these controversial texts as Paul's attempt to foster dignity in subordinate persons within ancient society, cultivate mutuality within socially stratified relationships, and encourage movement toward freedom within an unjust social order. He defines revolutionary subordination as "willing servanthood in the place of domination [which] enables the person in a subordinate position in society to accept and live within that status without resentment at the same time that it calls upon the person in the superordinate position to forsake or renounce all domineering use of that status."[38]

This concept is transformative in at least two ways. First, servanthood is a particular virtue that involves choosing solidarity with the least of these when the alternative is dominating them. To be a servant in the way of Jesus then is to explicitly reject the temptation to carry out his ministerial vision through oppressive and violent structures, consciously accepting "the cross" over "the crown."[39] Second, revolutionary subordination calls those at the top of the social order to renounce their power at the same time as it "assigns *personal moral responsibility to those who had no legal or moral status* in their culture and makes of them decision makers."[40] Christ's call to a peculiar servanthood enables the subordinate person to be free within an unjust order, even as it calls people at the top of the social hierarchy to change their behavior and lower their position in the hierarchy.[41] Like the slave Onesimus who returns to Philemon "'no longer as a slave, but . . . as a beloved brother, both in the flesh and in the Lord,'"[42] revolutionary subordination transforms relationships between oppressed and oppressor. In spite of its potential for resisting domination and equalizing relationships, however, revolutionary subordination appears to be inherently oppressive when Yoder asserts that it also calls people at the bottom of society to accept their disadvantaged position.

Although Yoder demonstrates how slaves, wives, and children in early Christian communities developed a sense of purpose and agency when they saw their status as "meaningful before God,"[43] it is nonetheless difficult to see how this aspect of revolutionary subordination can be liberating. Indeed, people were angered and offended by the idea, with feminist Elizabeth Schüssler Fiorenza openly criticizing Yoder for defending "the New Testament pattern of patriarchal submission."[44] Yet, this argument for revolutionary subordination must be examined in its context. In *The Politics of Jesus*, Yoder is addressing those scholars who view Ephesians 5:21–6:9 and Colossians 3:18–4:1 as indisputable signs of Jesus' irrelevance to social ethics and of the early Christians' subsequent need to adopt ethical practices from Stoic philosophy instead of the gospel. In response, Yoder contends that, far from a blind acceptance of social mores, early Christians were creatively helping those experiencing injustice to see that Christ has already liberated them and that the resurrection has already defeated the old hierarchical order. Revolutionary subordination then urges each undervalued person in the believing community to become "a *free ethical agent* in the act of voluntarily acceding to subordination in the power of Christ instead of bowing to it either fatalistically or resentfully."[45] Furthermore, it gives them "responsibility for viewing their status in society not as a simple meaningless decree of fate but . . . as an issue about which they can make a moral choice."[46]

One example of free moral agency in the midst of subordination is

Jesus' instruction to go the extra mile in the Beatitudes. In this instance, the person who is being molested accepts that he is in no position to over-power or refuse a soldier that coerces him to carry his pack. Despite these conditions, the abused person retains the ability to be a decision maker in choosing to carry the pack for another mile. While this action does not threaten the soldier's authority, look like resistance, or confront the polit-ical system that makes the abuse possible, the subordinated person exer-cises his will and freedom in Christ nevertheless and preserves his person-hood as a result. Like Jesus' listeners, Black people employed similar strategies for retaining their humanity during their brutal enslavement in the United States. Slaves engaged in acts of "simultaneous accommoda-tion and resistance,"[47] including working slowly in the fields, running away for short periods despite the threat of violence, singing spirituals that used biblical imagery to denounce their masters and communicate a desire for freedom, and many others. On one hand, these actions created space for slaves to reclaim their humanity together. On the other hand, these activities were also used to justify the slavery institution. For example, while pretending to be clumsy, stupid, or insane provided occasional relief from backbreaking labor, such actions inadvertently but unsurprisingly strengthened Whites view that "African-Americans suffered from special diseases . . . that caused Blacks to 'break, waste, and destroy everything they handle.'"[48] Similarly, slaves who sang, danced, and rattled their chains to "keep down trouble and keep our hearts from being completely broken" also supported the myth of the happy slave.[49] Black preachers in slave com-munities also had to maintain a delicate balance between accommodation and resistance. Like Paul writing to Ephesians and Colossians, they had to "speak a language defiant enough to hold the high-spirited among their flock but neither so inflammatory as to rouse them to battles they could not win nor so ominous as to arouse the ire of ruling powers. . . . The slave com-munities . . . counseled a strategy of patience, of acceptance of what could not be helped, of dogged effort to keep the black community alive and healthy."[50]

At this point, it is crucial to note that Yoder did not see limited resist-ance and accommodation as the only responses to oppression. Although he sees revolutionary subordination as a way for dominated persons to assert the freedom they discover in the gospel, he also argues that, "the Christian is called to view social status from the perspective of *maximizing freedom.*"[51] Therefore, "One who is given an opportunity to exercise more

freedom should do so, because we are all called to freedom in Christ. . . .
Yet, that freedom can already become real within one's present status by
voluntarily accepting subordination in view of the relative unimportance
of such social distinctions when seen in the light of the coming fulfillment
of God's purposes."[52] In other words, revolutionary subordination is not
static. It entails a series of movements, from oppressed persons learning to
live freely as people who are valued by Christ in situations that they are
unable to change to people seeking more freedom when opportunities
arise. To return to the example of slavery, Black people practiced revolutionary subordination when they resisted their oppression within the
entrenched plantation system and when they took available opportunities
to escape.

Viewed from a womanist perspective, revolutionary subordination
has transformative potential for Black women because it advocates seizing opportunities for greater liberation. During slavery, Sojourner Truth
embodied this concept when she changed her slave name to one of her
choice, signaling her freedom from bondage, and when she helped fellow slaves flee to freedom.[53] Today, revolutionary subordination for
Black women entails resisting patriarchy and racism by redefining what
it means to be "Black" and to be "woman." It involves calling Black
men into mutual relationships and shared leadership in churches. It
means speaking up for ourselves when we are exploited and embracing
our God-given selves when society pressures us to accept its standards
of womanhood. Most importantly, it entails living out Christ's liberating work within the reconciled community where there is no Jew or
Greek, male or female, slave or free.

Limitations of Revolutionary Subordination

While revolutionary subordination is helpful to Black women and
other subjugated groups, it is not without limitations. First, I believe the
term *revolutionary subordination* itself is an obstacle to understanding
Yoder's argument. Although the play on words is meant to reflect the
particular type of revolution Jesus models—one that triumphs over evil
without using violence and creates a reconciled community without
domination—common understandings of *revolution* and *subordination*
make it easy to dismiss Yoder's interpretation of those words. For example, if one defines revolution as overturning an undesirable social structure and exchanging it for a more just order, it is difficult to see turning

the other cheek or feigning insanity as revolutionary in part because these acts can bolster the oppressive system. Similarly, subordination carries an almost insurmountable negative connotation, no matter how it is defined. Even Yoder seems to recognize this hurdle as he cautions readers not to equate subordination with submission (passivity) or subjection (being "thrown down and run over").[54] Despite his best attempts, I think the word combination undercuts the nuances of his argument. Since the aforementioned forms of resistance by slaves and other oppressed people are at best imaginative forms of day-to-day resistance, a more positive and understandable term like "creative transformation"[55]—which Yoder also uses—might be more helpful.

My second critique of revolutionary subordination is that it seems to overlook the place for challenging the systems of power that dominate. To be fair, Yoder explicitly states that he is not mainly concerned with "the history of Christianity as a force for social justice"[56] in this particular study. In addition, his primary purpose for the chapter on revolutionary subordination in *The Politics of Jesus* is demonstrating that the gospel did indeed provide the lower classes with a "message affirming the dignity of the subordinate one."[57] Nevertheless, the question remains: is it enough to accept "an *order*, as it exists, but with the new meaning given to it by the fact that one's acceptance of it is willing and meaningfully motivated?"[58] Does not maximizing one's freedom also entail making an effort to transform the social order that makes continued oppression possible? Since challenging oppressive systems can easily fall into the "Constantinian" trap whereby Christians attempt to steer the course of history by assuming the crown, advocating violence or supporting the politics of the state, it is easy to see why Yoder would focus on exploring the transformative power of revolutionary subordination. Yet it seems to me that the maximizing freedom aspect of revolutionary subordination/creative transformation can also involve public, nonviolent resistance to domination in the way of the cross.

Martin Luther King Jr. is one example of the kind of revolutionary subordination/creative transformation that simultaneously accepts and redefines one's position in the social order *and* seeks to maximize people's freedom by confronting that social order's injustice. Despite the violence committed against Black people and the pervasive racist rhetoric about their inferiority, King did not hesitate to identify himself as a Black man and to stand in solidarity with the Black community. This is significant par-

ticularly because, as Yoder noted, King was "equipped with cultural information and educational credentials in order to understand the white
world"[59] and as such could have avoided struggle in the streets with his
peers. Subsequently, "his choice to return to the south and accept the pastoral leadership of the Dexter Avenue Baptist Church was a voluntary act
of identification with the cause of oppressed Black Americans"[60] that culminated in protest and petition for his and other Black people's freedom.
The "Black consciousness era"[61] in which people adopted personal, public
"symbols of Blackness"[62] is another example of revolutionary subordina-
tion/creative transformation that cannot be separated from social resistance. The voluntary adoption of Afros, dashikis, and other elements of
Black identity that were despised by White society not only enabled individuals to be free within a web of racist laws, policies, and practices; it also
fueled a desire to dismantle these structures. These two examples confirm
what Yoder recognized: that willing appropriation and reinterpretation,
accommodation and resistance are not the same as accepting ones inferior
status.[63] But they also show that revolutionary subordination/creative
transformation can intersect with a larger call for social renewal that follows in the footsteps of Jesus.

Conclusion

In spite of a few shortcomings, Yoder's theology of the cross offers
important challenges and integral support to the womanist project of naming Black women's struggles and redefining the cross in light of their suffering. By identifying the particular type of suffering in the cross, Yoder
helps to undercut the hermeneutics of sacrifice that has saturated Black history and persisted into the present. By articulating a notion of revolutionary subordination, Yoder provides additional tools to liberate Black
women even in the midst of oppression and adds theological support for
us to maximize our freedom. Although this conversation between womanist and Yoderian theology is not without its tensions, especially with regard
to the application of cross language and the place for public, social resistance within revolutionary subordination, they nevertheless reinforce and
compliment one another. Together these theologies serve Black women
well as we forge our identities, change our communities and attempt to
make our voices heard through the power of Jesus, who upholds us and
stands in solidarity with us.

Notes

1. JoAnne Marie Terrell, *Power in the Blood? The Cross in the African American Experience* (Maryknoll, NY: Orbis Books, 1998), 6.

2. Kelly Brown Douglas, *The Black Christ* (Maryknoll, NY: Orbis Books, 1994), 21. See also J. Albert Harrill, "The Use of the New Testament in the American Slave Controversy: A Case History in the Hermeneutical Tension between Biblical Criticism and Christian Moral Debate," *Religion and American Culture* 10, no. 2 (2000): 149-86.

3. Terrell, *Power in the Blood?*, 16.

4. Ibid., 22 (emphasis added).

5. Ibid., 19, 21 and 47.

6. Douglas, *The Black Christ*, 21.

7. Ibid., 25.

8. Terrell, *Power in the Blood?*, 30.

9. Ibid., 29.

10. Delores S. Williams, *Sisters in the Wilderness: The Challenge of Womanist God-Talk* (Maryknoll, NY: Orbis Books, 1993), 162.

11. Ibid., 60-61.

12. Ibid., 61.

13. Human Rights Watch, "Punishment and Prejudice: Racial Disparities in the War on Drugs," Vol. 12, No. 2, May 2000, http://www.hrw.org/reports/2000/usa/Rcedrg00-01.htm#P181_32502 (accessed December 10, 2006).

14. Chisun Lee, "Domestic Disturbance: The Help Set Out to Help Themselves," *Village Voice*, March 13–19, 2002, http://www.villagevoice.com/2002-03-12/news/domestic-disturbance/1 (accessed October 5, 2008).

15. Douglas, *The Black Christ*, 91.

16. Frances E. Wood, "Take My Yoke Upon You," in *A Troubling in my Soul: Womanist Perspectives on Evil and Suffering*, ed. Emilie M. Townes (Maryknoll, NY: Orbis Books: 1993), 39-40.

17. Ibid., 41-42.

18. Randall Kenan, "The Strange and Tragic Ballad of Mabel Pearsall," in *Let the Dead Bury Their Dead* (New York: Harcourt Brace Janovich, Publishers, 1992), 131, 134.

19. Ibid., 166.

20. Ibid.

21. Ibid., 165. Williams describes Jesus' ministerial vision as reconciling "body (individual and community), mind (of humans and of tradition) and spirit" (165) through information "an ethical ministry of words . . . a healing ministry of touch and being touched . . . a militant ministry of expelling evil forces . . . a ministry grounded in the power of faith . . . a ministry of prayer [and] a ministry of compassion and love" (167).

22. Jacquelyn Grant, *White Women's Christ and Black Women's Jesus: Feminist Christology and Womanist Response* (Atlanta: Scholars Press, 1989), 217.

23. Demetrius K. Williams, "Identifying with the Cross of Christ," in *The Passion of Our Lord: African American Reflections* (Minneapolis: Fortress Press, 2005), 85, 101-3.

24. Ibid., 90.

25. John Howard Yoder, *The Politics of Jesus*, 2nd ed. (Grand Rapids, MI: Eerdmans, 1994), 129.

26. John Howard Yoder, "The Power Equation, Jesus and the Politics of King," in *For the Nations: Essays Evangelical and Public* (Grand Rapids, MI: Eerdmans 1997), 143-44.

27. Yoder, *The Politics of Jesus*, 129.

28. Ibid., 96.

29. Ibid, 36.

30. Yoder, "The Power Equation," 145-46.

31. Terrell, *Power in the Blood?*, 2.

32. Douglas, *The Black Christ*, 22.

33. Williams, *Sisters in the Wilderness*, 169.

34. Jacquelyn Grant, "Womanist Jesus and the Mutual Struggle for Liberation," in *The Recovery of Black Presence: An Interdisciplinary Exploration*, ed. Randall C. Bailey and Jacquelyn Grant (Nashville: Abingdon Press, 1995), 139.

35. Yoder, *The Politics of Jesus*, 125.

36. Grant, *White Women's Christ and Black Women's Jesus*, 215.

37. Ibid., 212.

38. Yoder, *The Politics of Jesus*, 186.

39. Ibid., 35.

40. Ibid., 172.

41. Ibid., 177-78.

42. Ibid., 177.

43. Ibid., 172.

44. Elizabeth Schüssler Fiorenza, *Bread Not Stone: The Challenge of Feminist Biblical Interpretation* (Boston: Beacon Press, 1984), 83.

45. Yoder, *The Politics of Jesus*, 186 (emphasis added).

46. Ibid., 172.

47. Eugene Genovese, as quoted in Howard Zinn, *A People's History of the United States: 1492—Present*, rev. and updated ed. (New York: Harper Perennial, 1995), 170.

48. William Loren Katz, *Eyewitness: A Living Documentary of the African American Contribution to American History*, rev. and updated ed. (New York: Touchstone, 1995), 106.

49. John Little, as quoted in Zinn, *A People's History of the United States*, 168.

50. Eugene Genovese, as quoted in ibid, 173.

51. Yoder, *Politics of Jesus*, 182 (emphasis added).

52. Ibid., 182.

53. Terrell, *Power in the Blood?*, 17.

54. Yoder, *The Politics of Jesus*, 172.

55. Ibid., 185.

56. Ibid., 173.

57. Ibid., 175.

58. Ibid., 172.

59. John Howard Yoder, Poland Lecture Series, Warsaw, Poland 1983. Unpublished.

60. Ibid.

61. Douglas, *The Black Christ*, 35.

62. Ibid.

63. Yoder, *Politics of Jesus*, 181.

Chapter 6

Governmentality, Witness, and the State:

Christian Social Criticism with and Beyond Yoder and Foucault

Richard Bourne

This essay will outline a triptych of the theology of governmental power and of Christian witness to the state as found in John Howard Yoder's theology. Only two panels of this triptych are explicit in Yoder's writings; these I label *eschatology* and *exile*. In relation to these, I will claim that Michel Foucault gives us resources for understanding non-Constantinian forms of political critique. I then conclude by arguing that Yoder intimates toward, but failed to elaborate, a third panel; that of *election*. I do not intend merely to exposit parallels between two "thinkers." Such an undertaking would be neither useful nor particularly interesting. The thrust of the essay is not to explore the relation between Yoder's theology and Foucault's political thought but to show how Yoder and Foucault may help the church to be "more truly political . . . [a] more properly ordered community, than is the state."[1]

Throughout this essay, I contend that the three panels of this triptych impact the claims and concerns that orient contemporary political theory. Eschatology will be shown to offer a critique of notions of legitimacy. Exile brings into question excessive concerns with governmental sovereignty. Election contrasts with the pathological tendencies in modern Western notions of voluntariety as the key to popular sovereignty.

Eschatology and the Crisis of Legitimation[2]

In expressing the uncertainty of discerning the victory of God in the present, the author of the letter to the Hebrews nonetheless reassures us that we see in Jesus the just politics that only comes with the eschatological sovereignty of God (Heb 2:8-9). Christ is seated at the right hand of the Father. He is not simply intercessor or advocate, for his reign extends beyond the heart of the individual believer. To be seated beside the King is to take on the role of prime minister, the one who governs over the principalities and powers.[3] Yoder claims, with respect to Romans 13, that God has not created, instituted, or ordained the powers, but has *ordered* them according to his providential purpose.[4] It is within Pauline exousiology, the doctrine of the status and nature of these principalities and powers, that the claims of eschatology impinge upon the exercise of governmental power. The language of the powers provides an important means of analyzing the persistence of evil and the "spirituality" of social structures. Significantly, it is in employing this language that Yoder seeks to deny any competing (non-pacifist) ethical norm locating the political in the order of natural law.[5]

While most references to the powers consider them in their fallen state, this should not be allowed to obscure their basis in the creative purposes of God (Col 1:15-17). Since the victory of Christ, the powers are subject to God's providential sovereignty. They, like all creation, are caught in a time of eschatological tension. "The cosmic powers will not be destroyed, but they will be tamed, as they too will find their place in the new humanity."[6] This implies two things: first that "we cannot live without them" (yet, because they harm and enslave us, we cannot fully live with them); and second, that it is not the duty of the church to attack the powers, for "this Christ has done. The church concentrates upon not being seduced by them. By existing the church demonstrates that their rebellion has been vanquished."[7]

Yoder suggests that Pauline exousiology provides a structural analogy with contemporary phenomena. This is an analogical relation, not a simple identification. It thereby allows us to avoid dangerous claims about the naturalness of state operations, such that abstractions like *state, sovereignty,* or *legitimacy* are identified as necessary or permanent forms of the powers. Regnant structures are not the only way things can be. By rejecting "natural law" as a basis for a theology of the state Yoder does not downplay the importance of creation but provides a christological negation of early mod-

ern notions, from Bodin to Hobbes, of the nation-state as the natural product of social will. Such accounts perpetuate an idolatrous assertion of sovereign power as independent of eschatological claims.[8] For some critics, the
separation from eschatological reality found in the notion of popular sovereignty provides the "necessary historical condition of modern political
tyranny and totalitarianism."[9] In the rise of nation-states social space
becomes unified. The complexities of diverse claims upon a person's loyalties are vitiated by the supervenient claims of state sovereignty.

So how might Yoder's eschatology and exousiology relate to concerns for "legitimacy" in political theory? Yoder's most important claim
regarding legitimacy is stark—"Christian witness does not provide any
foundations for government, either practically or philosophically, but . . .
the Christian rather accepts the powers that be and speaks to them in a
corrective way."[10] This is the political equivalent to Yoder's christologically circumscribed methodological historicism, which clearly states that
"there is no scratch from which to start."[11] Political witness must begin
in the messy middle. Yoder was rightly impatient with theorizations and
abstractions that aimed at prior "semantic or definitional moves" ensur-
ing some neutral or universal site to begin discussion.[12] For our purposes
those abstractions would include "the state of nature," and the common-
place polarity of "anarchy" and "totalitarianism"—between which
extremes some "legitimate" state might rest. Thus Yoder insists that "the
witness to the state has never been *based on* a theory about what the
state is and should be in itself, nor has it been rendered *for the sake* of
the state 'in itself.'"[13] It is false to assume that "if one does not have a
theory justifying the existence of government one has no grounds for
criticizing governmental performance. . . . The state does not need to be
theoretically justified in order to exist; it does exist."[14]

Yoder's work provides an alternative to those forms of political theology that see their task in terms largely borrowed from the political dilemmas
addressed by Hobbes, Locke, and other harbingers of the liberal tradition—
i.e., the need to provide some thinly theologized grounds for sovereignty
and the legitimacy of the nation-state. Equally, we should note a significant
contrast with one of the most robust theological accounts of legitimate
political judgment—that of Oliver O'Donovan, for whom the fundamental
issue is the emergence of less theological (indeed actively de-theologizing)
notions of legitimacy after Grotius. These notions become idolatrous when
straying beyond the bounds of Christ's "reauthorization" of the state's judg-

ment.[15] The problem for Yoder is not simply that the state becomes idolatrous by straining at its eschatological leash. The fundamental error occurs when eschatology is turned inside-out, and the state is said to show forth Christ's sovereignty in its own actions in a way that is more truly "political" than the life of the believing community.

Yoder raises a number of objections to language of legitimacy. He contrasts two customary readings of Romans 13—the "positivistic" and the "legitimistic" or normative view.[16] The positivistic approach is characterized by an attempt to render an affirmative moral judgment on the existence of the current government by virtue of its very occurrence. "If Germany finds itself under the control of Adolf Hitler, this very fact demonstrates that his government is 'of God.'"[17] This abhorrent conclusion should be more than enough to dismiss such an approach. Nevertheless, more subtle forms of positivistic logic in the guise of a historic appeal to particular patterns of governance (as self-evidently effective, and therefore preferable) still permeate the rhetoric of both conservative retrograde politics, and, conversely, of "revolutionary" utopianism.

The legitimistic reading of Romans 13 is perhaps more attractive for those seeking a theological basis for social and political criticism. Yoder locates the reading within a broadly Calvinistic tradition, flowing from Zwingli, through Cromwell, and on to Barth and Brunner. "What is ordained is not a particular government but the concept of proper government, the principle of government as such."[18] Each particular constellation of governmental power is subject to critique on the basis of a prior standard. Should one's state be found wanting in its performance of the essential tasks of maintaining peace and punishing evildoers, or if it aggregates the kind of all-encompassing role found in totalitarian regimes, then the duty of the Christian is to revolt. Here Yoder demurs. Romans 13, he claims, cannot be used to justify revolt. The duty of the Christian is to remain subordinate to the state, no matter how unjust that state may be. Thus, "No state can be so low on the scale of relative justice that the duty of the Christian is no longer to be subject; no state can rise so high on that scale that Christians are not called to some sort of suffering because of their refusal to agree with its self-glorification and the resultant injustices."[19]

On the face of it, this is hardly the stuff of a theology capable of significant political critique. Indeed, here we encounter an ambiguity particularly characteristic of Yoder's earlier writings. The ambiguity revolves around the verbs "to be subject," and "to revolt." To avoid any patrician or positivistic misconstrual Yoder argues that Romans 13 then functions not as a legitimation of certain norms of government but as a counsel for "revolutionary subordination." He offers an important distinction that emphasizes both the voluntariety and the eschatological basis of radical Christian politics. "The term *hypotassesthai* is not best rendered by subjection, which carries a connotation of being thrown down and run over, nor by submission, with its connotation of passivity. Subordination means the acceptance of an order, as it exists, but with the new meaning given to it by the fact that one's acceptance of it is willing and meaningfully motivated."[20] To reject "legitimism" is only to reject the implicit imperative to violent rebellion.[21]

Yoder claims, "'subordination' is itself the Christian form of rebellion. It is the way we share in God's patience with a system we basically reject."[22] Eschatology is the key to understanding how the Church is to respond to God's providential *ordering* of the powers—whether they are "legitimate" or not!

Despite his unease with the term, I suggest Yoder's cause would have been better served by a more explicit delineation of a "functional" from an "ontological" sense of a state's legitimacy. He is persuasive in his critique of the monolithic sense of legitimacy. Yoder's theology of witness does not require one to reject *all* activities of a particular state, or accept them *all*.[23] He is also rightly cautious of the way language of legitimacy may base itself on an implied claim to attain an unrealistic level of clarity in judgment. There is no simple checklist, no unequivocal signal that allows us "to tell accurately the specific point at which a state would move from sobriety into idolatry."[24] For Yoder, the language of legitimacy runs the risk of imposing a simplistic polarity upon an infinitely complex setting.

However, this does not mean that language of legitimacy must be rejected—rather it may be useful, within certain limitations, as a means of addressing concrete issues. The functional norms applying to the state are defined in relation to the eschatological and christological vision from which Yoder's theology of witness stems.[25] The option is not between the legitimate government of Romans 13, which Christians are to bless, or the idolatrous government of Revelation 13, which should be overturned. For most biblical translations, the functional nature of this norm is compromised by reading Romans 13:6 along rather static ontological lines—"the authorities *are* God's servants, busy with this very thing." By contrast, for

Yoder the state has no ontology in and of itself; the exercise of authority is only in the service of God *to the extent that* it fulfils these minimal functions.[26] There is no such thing as the state *as such*. The state exists only as a permissive ordinance of God, with no ontology above or beyond the particular constellation of governmental activities exercised in its name. Thus, both Yoder and Barth can say that the New Testament contains no doctrine of the just state.[27]

Our subordination to a government is not conditional upon its putative legitimacy; but the same cannot be said of our obedience to that ruler! We can, and sometimes must, enact our subordination through disobedience. Yoder's disavowal of the abstract or ontological functioning of the term *legitimate* allows him to maintain that the illegitimate state, no less than the legitimate one, exists solely by divine patience. We should not deny that God's sovereign purposes may be served even through a morally abhorrent regime. YHWH's use of the idolatrous Assyria or Rome is not a ratification of their legitimacy.[28] Those nations may serve the purposes of God, but in no way does this exonerate them from his judgment.

Ontologically speaking, no state is entirely legitimate or illegitimate—for the state no longer has an existence outside of the order of grace, and no authority outside the lordship of Christ. The state belongs to the "order of providence," while the church belongs to the "order of redemption." The violence of the state is turned against itself in the kingdom of Christ. There are better or worse state forms. Even in its most democratized form the state can never escape a moment of self-deification.[29] So Yoder's eschatology and exousiology show us that the concept of legitimacy must be shorn of all ontological, abstract forms; it must not be taken to circumscribe God's free permissive action and patience; and it must be adequately distanced from connotations of moral ratification—only then is there some use for the term. The church's witness may utilize the language of legitimacy in a way that better fits the complexities of citizenship. Too often political theology juxtaposes accounts of state authority as requiring either subjection or rebellion—as if "sovereign power" were held by a singular, discrete and identifiable body. That is, and has always been, a myth—and often an idolatrous one at that. Yoder's eschatological vision undermines such bald polarities while still permitting a functional account of legitimacy that may allow the church to witness effectively to Christ's own sovereign lordship.[30]

Exile, Sovereignty and "Governmentality"

In later years Yoder's ecclesiology was increasingly expressed in terms of exilic citizenship.[31] Yoder gives an account of exile as both normative and as a blessing. The sense of radical dependence on YHWH that marks the identity of Israel is fundamental to their ability to live in exile. This dependence is a refusal of strategic manipulation of space as territory (the very ground for the claimed sovereignty of a nation-state) or the reification or commodification of divine presence. Thus the Mosaic tradition always insisted upon the mobility of the tabernacle as the representation of divine presence. In Yoder's words "[t]he transcendence of the Most High is acted out in the fact that the place of his manifestation is not our own turf."[32] "Judaism" and "Christianity" share a non-sovereign, non-territorial self-definition.[33]

Of course, exile entails suffering and loss. Yet, in no way does this diminish the constructive rhetoric of Jeremiah's prophecy—the exile is an occasion for the continued mission of the chosen people of God.[34] Exile is not a temporary punitive hiatus from which a swift return would mark the recommencement of the monarchic project—but for Yoder is a judgment upon the notions of sovereignty and territoriality found in that strand of thought. Exile continues the electing promise made to Abraham in Genesis 12:3. Israel is a peoplehood constituted not by the centripetal force of shared ethnicity, location, or political sovereignty; but by the centrifugal operation of divine blessing. The diaspora people of God make their contribution without engaging in the machinations of power politics. For Yoder, "not being in charge of the civil order is sometimes a more strategic way to be important for its survival or its flourishing than to fight over the throne. In dramatic and traumatic cases the Jews were murdered or banished; in more, quieter cases they were needed and appreciated despite (or thanks to) their nonconformity."[35]

Yoder is frequently falsely accused of an exclusively negative reading of the state.[36] This negativity is neither exclusive nor paralyzing. It does not yield any paralysis or stultification of action. Indeed it impels a discernment of degrees of better or worse government. This is no persistent naysaying, for a constructive and critical moment is always present. Likewise, Michel Foucault was often accused of a paralyzing negativity in his various accounts of the operations of power. I suggest that Yoder's exilic ecclesiology provides grounds for a form of Christian witness not only to "the state," but also to the wider functionings of power that Foucault diagnosed and named governmentality.

Foucault's characteristic focus on the way all discourses exercise forms of power that constrain and discipline their subjects was frequently misconstrued as providing a bleak picture of inescapably oppressive rationalities. Yet Foucault's oft-quoted response was "My point is not that everything is bad, but that everything is dangerous, which is not exactly the same as bad. If everything is dangerous, then we always have something to do. So my position leads not to apathy but to hyper- and pessimistic activism."[37] There are significant parallels between some accounts of the Pauline exousiology and Foucault's language here. Activism, for Foucault, is fostered in the discernment of the dangers inherent in all "technologies of the self."[38] These technologies take on multifarious forms, each exerting disciplinary power. For Foucault, the state exists solely as a constellation of these technologies. In his terms it is a "composite reality" and a "mythicised abstraction."[39]

This compliments our previous insistence that the state has no ontology in and of itself. Foucault argued that the state, as a discrete entity, has been afforded far too much attention. His famous aphorism that "in political theory we are yet to cut off the King's head" should be taken as an endeavor to broaden the examination of the operation of power and domination beyond concerns for sovereignty and obedience.[40] Government "is not just a power needing to be tamed or an authority needing to be legitimized. It is an activity and an art which concerns all and which touches each."[41] In modern Western civilization, techniques of domination interact with techniques of the self. External dominating practices are combined with an increasing level of self-government.[42]

The notion of governmentality springs from Foucault's response to critics for whom his writings, in their focus on specific events and genealogies, failed to account for the important role played by larger political systems like the state. Foucault's reply took the characteristic form of the exposure and denial of the supposedly self-evident importance of the state-form.[43] Foucault defined government simply and profoundly as "the conduct of conduct." Practices of government shape the field of action. Social critique therefore needs to be aware of the ubiquity of the disciplinary power through which persons and communities are placed in this field of action. That, of course, is the crux of Foucault's project—to enable dissent, to resist "what is," to encourage a "political spirituality."[44]

The genealogy of modern state power is traced to the "demonic" confluence of the Hebraic form of pastoral power (the shepherd-flock game) with the Greek civic model (the city-citizen game).[45] In modernity the state aggregates both an individualizing and a totalizing role.[46] That is to say, without conscious recognition of any inherent tensions, modern governmental rationality frames both the formation of the self and the nation. It is the understanding of the art of governing persons and populations. Put simply, government comes to name the process by which the social is created as secure *and* the individual is created as free. Biopolitics, Foucault's term for that enormous terrain on which governance is exercised upon bodies (both somatic and social), emerges in line with the problematization of "populations."[47] It is population, and not geographical territory, that is the prime object of governmental activity. We might say that, though pastoral power is itself transformed in the process, sovereignty is now exercised over the flock, not primarily the field.[48] The bio-political domain emerges at the threshold of modernity, and there it establishes an era of governmentality.

Both Foucault and Yoder, in different ways, bring into question any assumption that the supposedly cooperative basis of modern political society is free from moments of oligarchic rule. Yoder is quite clear that it has always been the case that "government" is more than just "the sword"—and that "when modern social orders assign to 'government' the administration of many other kinds of services, it is by no means necessary to apply to them all the same church/world dualism which the New Testament applied to servanthood and the sword."[49] Indeed, it is not often appreciated by Yoder's critics that active participation in wider functionings of government, including wider exercises of power are not necessarily and absolutely antithetical to the non-Constantinian witness of the diaspora community. Yoder argues,

> The assumption that commitment to a minority ethic, derived from a minority faith, must issue logically in withdrawal from significant involvement in the social process, including the refusal of office holders or adversary roles, is itself an outworking of the establishment axioms which I am challenging. It assumes . . . that the relevance of an ethical stance depends on the readiness of its constituency to fill *all* the posts in society. It assumes . . . that the paradigm of the exercise of social responsibility is not the civil servant or the opposition legislator, the minority agitator or the political prisoner, but the sovereign.[50]

In arguing this Yoder issues not a concession, but a challenge. With the "governmentalization of the state" the problem of sovereignty does not fade away, but becomes all the more acute.[51] Foucault argues that in the eighteenth century, "sovereignty" is a problem because it must now answer another set of questions than those addressed by Machiavelli. It is "no longer a question of . . . How to deduce an art of government from theories of sovereignty, but rather, given the existence and deployment of an art of government, what juridical form, what institutional form, and what legal basis could be given to the sovereignty typical of a state."[52] In resisting this Foucault sees the need to move beyond Leviathan and provide an antidisciplinary account of politics freed from the principle of sovereignty.[53]

In their appreciation for local practices of resistance both Yoder and Foucault argue for the independence of critical from constructive imperatives. Foucault's displacing of the sovereign as the subject of discourse on power strongly corresponds to Yoder's anti-Constantinian denial of Caesar as "the only mover of history."[54] Foucault denies the charges of paralysis and anesthesia, again turning the tables—"[t]he necessity of reform mustn't be allowed to become a form of blackmail serving to limit, reduce or halt the exercise of criticism."[55]

Foucault's thoroughgoing historicism contrasts here with Yoder's important christological circumscription of historical relativity. By contrast with Foucault's history of power, with its motifs of chance and arbitrary succession, we find in both Yoder's theology of the cross (with its revolutionary vision of powerlessness and patience in the face of contingency) and his exilic vision (with its emphasis on meaning in apparently powerless settings) a form of politics that refuses the absolute juxtaposition between revolution and reform. Critique and dissent are not just negative but are oriented by the pro in protest—for Christian protest the normative vision comes from the eschatological revelation of Christ as Lord.[56] Thus "a minority group with no immediate chance of contributing to the ways things go may still by its dissent maintain the wider community's awareness of some issues in such a way that ideas which are unrealistic for the present come to be credible later."[57] Both the operations of governmentality, and resistance to it, emerge in local, particular, and ad hoc ways.

The ethos of critique found in Foucault's understanding of governmentality is not primarily a patrician one. "Critique doesn't have to be the premise of a deduction which concludes: this then is what needs to be done. It should be an instrument for those who fight, for those who resist and refuse what is."[58] Equally, Yoder consistently rebuffs those who, through an imperative to the "responsible" presentation of constructive options, would confine pacifist witnesses to the margin of idealist conscience-pricking.[59] Indeed, Foucault's account of the local character of critique is expressed in an idiom that evokes strong associations with Yoder's normative vision of exilic citizenship. Foucault writes, "I think that the essentially local character of critique in fact indicates something resembling a sort of autonomous and non-centralized theoretical production, or in other words a theoretical production that does not need a visa from some common regime to establish its validity."[60] Nonetheless, one must be cautious in appropriating such parallels between Yoder and Foucault too quickly. Just as Yoder would not have endorsed all forms of nonviolent resistance, so too not all local practices would be acceptable—to be a critic of sovereignty is not necessarily to escape the danger of Constantinianism.

A Hint Toward the "Beyond"—Election and Voluntariety

I gave this essay the somewhat ambitious title of "Governmentality, Witness, and the State: Christian Social Criticism with *and Beyond* Yoder and Foucault." I now turn in somewhat brief and fragmentary fashion to one possible element of that "beyond." Both Foucault and Yoder have, in rather different ways, been accused of utilizing accounts of human freedom and possessive individualism that owe too much to the liberal modernist vision they eschew. Foucault, the arch-critic of all humanisms, still managed to write in favor of aspects of the Kantian vision.[61] Certainly there is a tension that we cannot explore here between the concern for (covertly liberal) defense of "freedom" in Foucault and his Nietzschean disdain for metaphysics.

Oliver O'Donovan argues that the critical potential of Yoder's thought is undermined by a "free-church" concern for the maintenance of uncoerced voluntariety. Yoder is said, somewhat unfairly, to conform the church to the model of a club or political party.[62] I suggest that a tacit and underdeveloped theology of election may be found in Yoder that counters such claims while also placing in question the modern political myth of voluntariety. Yoder's intention in arguing for the voluntary nature of the Christian community is not the preservation of individual rational freedom but the construction of a community of authentic nonviolent witness.[63] The presence of a committed community is an essential precondition for authentic protest.[64] To affirm the church as a *voluntary* community is to say that the grace present in coming to belief, mediated as it is by formational traditions, entails an aspect (not necessarily a discernible punctiliar moment) of conscious and deliberate submission to communal life. This decision is then enacted in the rite of baptism. The freedom of Christ is not the fabricated liberty of the consumer but the gracious embrace of the nonviolent life of the church.

Yoder's language of voluntariety is problematic. A modernist understanding of the abstract "will" does not undergird it, but that is a misunderstanding his work does little to avoid. Yoder is emphatic that apologetic attempts to render the Christian message credible in ways that sidestep the Jewishness of the promise in which the church's mission finds its guarantee, or "detached the message of Jesus from its Jewish matrix . . . thereby transposed it into an ahistorical moral monotheism with no particular peoplehood and no defenses against acculturation."[65] Thus Yoder links emergent supersessionism with the loss of critical ability. The proper functioning of the doctrine of election is as a missiological and ecclesiological category, rather than an abstract, individualized and ahistorical soteriology. As Barth rightly insisted in his creative reworking of the Calvinist approach, it is Christ who is the elect—and we who are incorporated into that election.[66] The election of Abraham, Isaac, and Jacob continues through the reconstitution of Israel around the person of Jesus, and, in and through him, is seen in the church.[67]

The doctrine of election allows us to see YHWH's choice of Israel, Jesus, and the church as the means by which the reconciliation of the world with God is wrought. As Colin Gunton puts it, "God elects the particular in order to achieve his universal purposes."[68] To affirm the aspect of voluntariety in ecclesial election does not negate the divine work of constituting the church. It is not the individual's or the community's act of gathering that, in and of itself, *constitutes* the church. Rather "the Spirit of God, acting through the word of God and the sacraments, is the real subject of the genesis of the church."[69] The act of constitution is not based in an ecclesiological form of the social contractarian theory.

This missiological understanding of ecclesial election is consistent with how the voluntary nonviolent community envisaged by Yoder provides a construction of "the social" that is able to ground a significant theological critique, indeed we can properly call it a "demythologization," of the modern state. The exilic community is the subject of God's elective blessing and thus the conduit of his reconciling purposes. It is not the individual believer who is elect but the community into which that believer is inducted in baptism. Election therefore differs from individual vocation in its ontological understanding of participation in Christ and incorporation into his body, the church. The motif of the elect community marks a contrast with the voluntarist and consumerist reading of popular sovereignty.

Together these three panels of the triptych—eschatology (exousiology), exile, and election provide critical moments in an account of the witness born by the church to the Lordship of Christ in an era of governmentality. When Yoder says that the church is more truly political than the state, that is a politics not defined by concerns for legitimacy, sovereignty, and government—but is instantiated in ways closer to Foucault's vision of politics as "no more or less than that which is born with resistance to governmentality."[70] The motifs of eschatology, exile, and election all militate against false resolutions and completeness. Modern political theory seeks to contain politics within the three concerns discussed—it locates legitimacy in the exercise of sovereign power in a way that flows from and itself enables the negative freedom of the self-possessing individual. Yoder's political theology isn't so much a competing schema as an unsettling of the enclosure of politics to the apparent givenness of such notions—in his words, "the new world or the new regime under which we live is not a simple alternative to present experience but rather a renewed way of living within the present."[71]

Notes

1. John Howard Yoder, *The Christian Witness to the State* (Newton, KS: Faith and Life Press, 1964), 18.

2. Jürgen Habermas, *Legitimation Crisis* (Oxford: Polity Press, 1988).

3. John Howard Yoder, *Preface to Theology: Christology and Theological Method* (Grand Rapids, MI: Brazos Press, 2002), 114-20.

4. John Howard Yoder, *The Politics of Jesus: Vicit Agnus Noster*, 2nd ed. (Grand Rapids, MI: Eerdmans, 1994), 201.

5. Yoder, *The Christian Witness to the State*, 33-4; *Politics*, 159.

6. John Howard Yoder, *He Came Preaching Peace* (Scottdale, PA: Herald Press, 1985), 114.

7. Yoder, *Politics*, 150.

8. Of course the emergence of the notion of legitimacy based in natural law progresses from the relatively complex and robustly theological Thomist framework through to more naturalistic (i.e. less Christocentric) accounts from the early seventeenth century. Hugo Grotius' attempts to place international order on the basis of a natural law, whose source remained God, but which proceeded by means of the emergence of a popular mandate—*De Iure Belli ac Pacis* book 1—may well have sewn the seeds for Hobbes' view of "natural law" no longer as the dictates of God, but the prudential exercise of reason discerning universal abstract laws like "Seek for Peace" and "don't do to others what you don't want done to you." Thomas Hobbes *Leviathan*, ch.14.

9. Joan Lockwood O'Donovan associates the view with figures as diverse as Hannah Arendt and Pope Leo XIII. "Nation, State and Civil Society in the Western Biblical Tradition" in Oliver O'Donovan and Joan Lockwood O'Donovan, *Bonds of Imperfection: Christian Politics, Past and Present* (Grand Rapids, MI: Eerdmans, 2004), 290. See also Oliver O'Donovan, *The Desire of the Nations: Rediscovering the Roots of Political Theology* (Cambridge, MA: Cambridge University Press, 1996), 49.

10. Yoder, *The Christian Witness to the State*, 41.

11. John Howard Yoder, *For the Nations: Essays Public and Evangelical* (Grand Rapids, MI: Eerdmans, 1997), 10.

12. Yoder, "On Not Being Ashamed of the Gospel: Particularity, Pluralism, and Validation," *Faith and Philosophy* 9, no. 3 (1992): 290-91.

13. Yoder, *The Christian Witness to the State*, 77.

14. Ibid., 78 n5.

15. See in particular O'Donovan, *The Desire of the Nations*, and *The Ways of Judgment* (Grand Rapids, MI: Eerdmans, 2005).

16. Yoder, *Politics*, 193-211.

17. Ibid., 199.

18. Ibid.

19. Yoder, *The Christian Witness to the State*, 77.

20. Yoder, *Politics*, 172.

21. Yoder, *The Christian Witness to the State*, 43.

22. Ibid., 200 n10.

23. Yoder, "Church and State According to a Free Church Tradition," in *On Earth Peace*, ed. Donald F. Durnbaugh (Elgin, IL: Brethren Press, 1978), 282.

24. Yoder, *The Christian Witness to the State*, 80.

25. Yoder, *The Original Revolution*, 76.

26. Yoder, *Politics*, 205.

27. Karl Barth, "The Christian Community and The Civil Community,"

in *Against the Stream: Shorter Postwar Writings, 1946-52* (London: SCM, 1954), 15-50.

28. Yoder, *Politics*, 198.

29. John Howard Yoder, *The Priestly Kingdom: Social Ethics as Gospel* (Notre Dame, IN: University of Notre Dame Press, 1985), 137; *The Christian Witness to the State*, 38; and *Karl Barth and the Problem of War, and other Essays on Barth*, ed. Mark Thiessen Nation (Eugene, OR: Wipf & Stock, 2003), 109.

30. Yoder, *The Christian Witness to the State*, 43-44.

31. I have discussed elsewhere the importance of this motif for an account of Christian witness in civil society. "Witness, Democracy and Civil Society: Reflections on John Howard Yoder's Exilic Ecclesiology," *Ecclesiology* 3, no. 2 (2007): 195-213.

32. John Howard Yoder, *The Jewish-Christian Schism Revisited* (Grand Rapids, MI: Eerdmans, 2003), 161-66.

33. Yoder, *The Royal Priesthood*, 133.

34. Yoder, *The Jewish-Christian Schism Revisited*, 199 n30.

35. Ibid., 172.

36. For example, such critiques fail to recognize the positive and con-structive tenor of Yoder's account of what he names William Penn's "Holy Experiment." Yoder, *Chapters in the History of Religiously Rooted NonViolence: A Series of Working Papers of the Joan B Kroc Institute for International Peace Studies*, unpublished papers 1996, ch. 7, available online at http://theology.nd.edu/people/research/yoder-john/documents/WILLIAMPENN.pdf; and Yoder, *For the Nations*, 20-21.

37. Michel Foucault, *The Essential Works 1954-84, vol. 1 Ethics, Subjectivity and Truth*, ed. Paul Rainbow (New York: The New York Press, 1997), 256.

38. Foucault, "Technologies of the Self" in *Essential Works 1954-84*, vol. 1, 223-51.

39. Foucault, "Governmentality," in *The Foucault Effect: Studies in Governmentality*, ed. Graham Burchell, Colin Gordon, and Peter Miller (Chicago: University of Chicago Press, 1991), 87-104.

40. Dean, *Governmentality*, 24-25, quoting Foucault, *Power/Knowledge* (New York: Pantheon, 1980), 121.

41. Burchell, Gordon, and Miller, *The Foucault Effect*, x.

42. Thomas Lemke, "'The Birth of Bio-Politics': Michel Foucault's Lecture at the Collège de France on Neo-Liberal Governmentality," in *Economy and Society* 30, no. 2 (2001): 190-207.

43. Colin Gordon, "Governmental Rationality: An Introduction," in Burchell, Gordon, and Miller, *The Foucault Effect*, 4.

44. "the will to discover a different way of governing oneself through

a different way of dividing up true and false—this is what I would call 'political *spiritualité*'" (Foucault, "Questions of Method," in Burchell, Gordon, and Miller, *The Foucault Effect*, 82).

45. Dean, *Governmentality*, 74-82, 96.

46. Michel Foucault, *Security, Territory, and Population: Lectures at the Collège de France*, trans. Graham Burchell (Basingstoke: Palgrave MacMillan, 2007).

47. Foucault, *Security, Territory,* and *Population and Ethics: Essential Works 1954-84*, 67-79.

48. Foucault, *Security, Territory and Population*, esp. 87-114.

49. Yoder, *The Priestly Kingdom*, 165.

50. Ibid., (emphasis added).

51. Foucault, *Governmentality*, 102.

52. Foucault, *Security, Territory and Population*, 106.

53. Michel Foucault, *Society Must be Defended: Lectures at the College de France 1975-1976* (London: Penguin, 2003), 34, 39-40.

54. John Howard Yoder, "Armaments and Eschatology," *Studies in Christian Ethics* 1, no. 1 (1988): 56.

55. Foucault, "Questions of Method" in Burchell, Gordon, and Miller, *The Foucault Effect*, 73-86.

56. Yoder, "Christianity and Protest in America," unpublished, 1991. Presented in November, 1991, at a conference on "Christianity and Democracy" convened at Emory University Law School with co-sponsorship of Pew Trust and the Association for Public Justice. Available online at http://theology.nd.edu/people/research/yoder-john/documents/CHRISTIANITYANDPROTESTINAMERICA.pdf

57. Yoder, *The Priestly Kingdom*, 96.

58. Foucault, "Questions of Method," 84.

59. Yoder, *The Priestly Kingdom*, 178-79.

60. Foucault, *Society Must Be Defended*, 6.

61. Michel Foucault, "What is Enlightenment?" in *The Foucault Reader: An Introduction to Foucault's Thought*, ed. Paul Rabinow (London: Penguin, 1986), 32-50.

62. O'Donovan, *The Desire of the Nations*, 223-24.

63. Yoder, *The Priestly Kingdom*, 105-13.

64. Yoder, "Christianity and Protest in America."

65. Yoder, *The Jewish-Christian Schism Revisited*, 152.

66. Karl Barth, *Church Dogmatics* II/2, trans. G. W. Bromiley & T. F. Torrance (Edinburgh: T & T Clark, 1956-1975), 94-127.

67. N. T. Wright, *Jesus and the Victory of God* (London: SPCK, 1996).

68. Colin Gunton, "Election and Ecclesiology in the Post-Constantinian Church," *Scottish Journal of Theology* 53, no. 2 (2000): 212-27.

69. Miroslav Volf, *After Our Likeness: The Church as the Image of the Trinity* (Grand Rapids, MI: Eerdmans, 1998), 176ff.

70. Foucault, *Security, Territory, Population*, 390.

71. Yoder, *Politics*, 185. These claims receive a deeper and more detailed treatment in my *Seek the Peace of the City: Christian Political Criticism as Public, Realist and Transformative* (Eugene, OR: Cascade, forthcoming).

Chapter 7

Not Engineering, But Doxology?
Reexamining Yoder's Perspective on the Church

Paul C. Heidebrecht

Engineers are not spoken of highly in the work of John Howard Yoder, to say the least. Engineering is characterized as being preoccupied with effectiveness and is thus contrasted with the kind of witness the church is called to embody. In short, for Yoder, Christians are called to proclaim, not to produce, the kingdom of God. After describing Yoder's criticism of engineering in the opening section, the second section of this essay goes on to argue that Yoder himself appears to betray the mind of a engineer. This becomes most clear when we shift our focus from his work on how the church is called to relate to the world to his work on the history of the church. Indeed, there appears to be a significant point of tension between Yoder's providential view of the world on the one hand and his "radical reformation" view of church history on the other. The third section will provide an enriched depiction of the practice of engineering, setting up the concluding section in which I argue that having the mind of an engineer is not necessarily a bad thing for a theologian, assuming that we correctly understand engineering as a practice more akin to artistry than science.

The overall argument of this essay may come as a surprise given its starting point: John Howard Yoder is appropriately characterized as an engineer of the church and is appropriately criticized when he is not a good enough engineer. Being pragmatic about the history and direction of the church is not necessarily problematic, provided we are prepared to acknowledge the ultimate mysteriousness of the way this history develops. Like Yoder, I think that both the faithfulness and the effectiveness of the church depend upon the working of God's Spirit in our midst. Going beyond Yoder, I think theologians can say much about the way this Spirit comes to form the followers of Christ.

Not Engineering

John Howard Yoder's pejorative use of the term *engineering* is quite striking. In every case that I am aware of in which Yoder invokes *engineering* or the phrase *to engineer*, he is contrasting engineering with his preferred stance or posture toward the world. That is, he is contrasting an engineering approach to the world with his concern to emphasize God's control of history, or, to put it more directly, the providence of God.

This negative portrayal of engineering is most obvious in one of the final chapters of the last collection of essays Yoder published before his sudden death in 1997.[1] Yoder's task in "Are You the One Who Is to Come?" is to reflect on the witness of the gospel regarding God's concern for, and participation in, human history. While he wants to avoid making "a few timeless generalizations about a vision for history," Yoder is convinced that the story of Jesus "implies and affirms deep certainties about God's intention for the human story."[2] The bottom line is that with Christ's resurrection the redemption of all of history has been secured; the final victory has been won. As followers of Jesus we are part of a community that is made possible by this victory, and thus "Our life is to proclaim, not to produce, the new world."[3]

Yoder begins to flesh out this catchy phrase in a section entitled "Not Engineering, but Doxology." Just what then does Yoder mean by engineering? While social ethics has typically been concerned with setting broad goals that describe the kind of world we want to live in, he tells us that engineering is "bringing to bear toward that end whatever power we have available." Put another way, he writes that engineering is what we are doing when we ask the question "How do we get from here to there?"[4] Yoder argues that Jesus was not interested in the questions of either engineering or modern social ethics but in asking a third question. Jesus was not asking what kind of world we want or how we can get it; he was asking how we can recognize the new world that has already been born in our midst: "How can the lordship of YHWH, affirmed in principle from all eternity, be worthily confessed as grace through faith? How can the present world be rendered transparent to the reality already there, that the sick are to be healed and the prisoners freed?"[5]

Once again, this is a point that Yoder makes in many different ways in many of his writings. The key point to note here is the terminology he uses in this particular case in order to provide a sharp contrast with the approach of Jesus. Yoder tells us that salvation is *not* a "product," it is a "presupposition"; it is *not* something that we "bring . . . about," it is something we "accept . . . as a gift." Likewise, shalom is *not* something we "achieve," it is something we "accept"; it is *not* something we "engineer," it is something we "proclaim." This list suggests that another definition of engineering for Yoder is to produce, to bring about, or to achieve something.

There are several additional references in *For the Nations* that provide further substance to Yoder's understanding of engineering. For example, in "The Racial Revolution in Theological Perspective," he correlates the Constantinian model for Christian ethics with "social engineering," since "thinking about right and wrong must now be tailored to fit everyone, singly and collectively."[6] And so, in addition to restating the more obvious connections between engineering and the pragmatist concern with "effectiveness,"[7] and with those who strive for actions that are "instrumental,"[8] Yoder implicates engineering in the modern impulse toward, to use one of his terms, "generalizability."[9] And yet he goes even further in this essay; engineering is also connected to those who focus on "theoretical sketches of the new order toward which we must move."[10] Thus for Yoder engineering is not just about trying to achieve an end in any way possible, it is about generalizing or standardizing—a one-size-fits-all approach to problem solving. And it is about theorizing and systematizing—an abstract and aloof approach to problem solving. It seems as though an engineer could serve as a good stand-in for Constantine as the chief symbol in Yoder's work for all that has gone wrong in the history of the church.

There are numerous additional references in Yoder's corpus that point to, or at least allude to, this pejorative view of engineering. To mention just one example, in *The Priestly Kingdom* Yoder lists "A New Value for Effectiveness" as one of six "Constantinian Sources of Western Ethics."[11] Here he is pointing to "the transformation of moral deliberation into utilitarianism," whereby "any ethic, any tactic, is . . . to be tested by its promised results." He refers to this as "the engineering approach to ethics," something that is "a long-range echo of the Constantinian wedding of piety with power."[12] After all, in biblical times it would have been senseless to think that a few powerless believers could ever promise, much less produce, results of any kind. And so in Yoder's view, the early followers of Jesus could never have had an engineering mindset.

An Engineer of the Church?

To be sure, there are times when Yoder actually demonstrated some enthusiasm for engineering-related work. For example, in the late 1970s Yoder joined a small group of Mennonite academics and development experts in starting a not-for-profit company called International Development Enterprises. The purpose of this organization was (and is) to connect Western technical expertise with needs in "third world" communities, and Yoder's correspondence related to this project demonstrates a surprising level of interest in technical details.[13]

Qualifications to Yoder's pejorative view of engineering can also be found in his published work. In another essay in *For the Nations*, "The Believer's Church and the Arms Race," he writes: "When I say we are free from the engineering model of the social process, that does not mean we stand its analysis on its head and say we don't care about planning, thinking, analyzing." Indeed, he insists that it is important to consider "mechanisms, causality, [and] probabilities" provided that this "fosters concern" rather than "despair."[14] And in "The Biblical Mandate for Evangelical Social Action," he insists that praising God does not mean we can avoid "the need to think practically, weighing likely effects and relative costs of available strategies."[15]

Further qualifications can be found in some of the words and phrases that Yoder uses to describe the way the church should relate to its surrounding society. In response to the charge that the vision of the church he describes is sectarian, at various times Yoder insisted that the church is: "the beginning, the *pilot run*, the *bridgehead* of the new world on the way";[16] God's *beachhead* in the world as it is; the downpayment, the *prototype*, the herald, the midwife of the new world on the way";[17] concerned for the *relative improvement* of society";[18] and "a ministry of *constant inventive vision* for the good of the larger society."[19]

Phrases like "relative improvement" and "constant inventive vision" evoke images of the church as a laboratory developing the next generation of a computer operating system. "Pilot run" and "prototype" evoke images of the church as a new vehicle design being driven off the assembly line for the first time, ready to be subjected to close scrutiny and possibly even some destructive testing. And of course "bridgehead" and "beachhead" evoke images of the church as a technological artifact of military significance.

Technological metaphors for the way the church works in the world aside, Yoder sounds rather pragmatic when he insists that the church "concentrates on the identification and removal of one abuse at a time rather than on theoretical sketches of the new order toward which we must move."[20] Furthermore, as much as Yoder relativizes the importance of instrumental thinking when it comes to societal practices, at times he seems to verge on instrumental thinking when it comes to ecclesial practices. The most obvious reference point is *Body Politics*, a book that was written to highlight the public witness of key church practices such as binding and loosing, the Eucharist, baptism, recognizing the multiplicity of gifts, and open meetings.[21] Yoder's non-sacramental, functional, or, as he put it, "moderately realistic"[22] view of church practices has already been subject to numerous challenges. Although I would take issue with some of these challenges, it is interesting that Yoder's focus on the socio-political dimension of church practices, much like his concern to identify and remove one abuse at a time, sounds like the church is "bringing to bear toward that end whatever power we have available." It sounds like the answer to the question "How do we get from here to there?" It sounds like something an engineer might say.

Even more significantly, however, throughout his work Yoder sounds like an engineer when he shifts his focus from the relationship of the church to the world, to the life of the church. For as much as he downplays the priority of mechanisms, causality, and probabilities when it comes to social history writ large, a case can be made that he is very interested in mechanisms, causality, and probabilities when it comes to church history. Indeed, it would appear there is a significant point of tension between Yoder's providential perspective on the history of the world and his interventionist perspective on the history of the church. Yoder's life work called the church to be more faithful in following Jesus Christ, pointing out where it had come close, where it had fallen short, and the direction it needed to go in the moment under consideration.

The clearest sign of this perspective is Yoder's "posture of radical reformation."[23] Certainly, as Yoder notes in *The Priestly Kingdom*, all Protestants are united by "the conviction that in the earlier history of Christianity something had gone wrong."[24] However, according to Yoder the correct response to this analysis is not to seek to return the church to its pre-fallen state as restitutionists insist, for "there will always have to be change."[25] The correct response is to recognize that the church is "not only fallible but in fact peccable."[26] Thus the church should be subjected to continuous, never-ending critique—to put it even stronger, it should embody "a constant potential for reformation, and in the more dramatic situations, a readiness for the reformation even to be 'radical.'"[27] As Yoder says:

> Checking how we went wrong and asking how to get back on track is thus not an odd emergency, a rare glitch along the triumphal way. . . Salvation becomes history not with the rigidity of the railroad, but with the balanced momentum of the bicycle or the walker. Every step calls for balance to be restored.[28]

Put another way: "Far from being an ongoing growth like a tree . . . the wholesome growth of a tradition is like a vine: a story of constant interruption of organic growth in favor of pruning and a new chance for the roots." As a result, the appeal to origins is properly seen to be "a 'looping back,' a glance over the shoulder to enable a midcourse correction."[29] And so Yoder's use of the image of a "vinedresser" reminds us that the potential for radical reformation is not only a critical, but a renewing posture.

The point to be emphasized here is that, whether the image is mechanistic or organic, Yoder was most definitely motivated by a desire to renew the church, both for the benefit of local congregations and for the sake of Christian unity. He constantly asked: "How did we get from there to here?" and "How do we get from here to there?" And he tried to encourage effective change in the church—to produce, achieve, or bring about a desired end—while recognizing that there will always be new challenges that cannot be anticipated in advance. It thus seems appropriate to go so far as to call Yoder an "engineer of the church."

Engineering, Properly Understood

Until now the discussion of engineering in this essay has been confined to the terms utilized by Yoder, although I have attempted to demonstrate that there are times when Yoder himself appears to betray the mind of an engineer according to these terms. In the following paragraphs I will sketch an enriched understanding of the practice of engineering, an understanding based on a loose consensus among a wide range of more philosophically-minded engineers. But before going any further it should be made clear that I will be talking about engineering as a *practice*, in the way that the philosopher Alasdair MacIntyre uses this word. That is, engineering—like architecture, farming, and football—is properly viewed as a practice because it is a "cooperative human activity" that develops over time in the threefold sense of achieving particular ends, cultivating particular skills in its practitioners, and making measured progress in these skills from generation to generation.[30] One advantage of viewing engineering as a practice is that it becomes possible to talk about engineers and the work of engineers in a collective way even though engineers do not typically comprise a clearly defined or autonomous group. It is also a broader term than knowledge-focused alternatives such as *discipline*, or organization-focused alternatives such as *profession*.

The crucial point I want to make about the practice of engineering is that while it is often preoccupied with effectiveness, it is *not* Constantinian. Engineering, properly understood, is *not* a one-size-fits-all, abstract, and aloof approach to problem solving; the practice of engineering does *not* hinge upon generalizations, or even on the application of theory.

A preoccupation with effectiveness can be seen clearly in most definitions of engineering. For example, the aeronautical engineer Walter Vincenti follows his colleague Gordon F. C. Rogers in defining engineering as "the practice of organizing the design and construction [and operation] of any artifice which transforms the physical world around us to meet some recognized need."[31] Like most people—including Yoder—for Rogers and Vincenti, engineering is all about producing, bringing about, or achieving something. This focus on getting the job done is echoed by the historian of technology and civil engineer Henry Petroski, who, by way of a quote from a nineteenth-century railroad engineer, defines engineering as "the art of doing well for one dollar what any bungler can do with two."[32]

A similarly pragmatic, yet more developed definition of engineering is provided by the nuclear engineer Billy Vaughn Koen, who defines the engineering method as "the strategy for causing the best change in a poorly understood situation within the available resources."[33] The key, of course, is fleshing out just what the strategy is for doing this. Koen argues that it is the use of heuristics, that is, "anything that provides a plausible aid or direction in the solution of a problem but is in the final analysis unjustified, incapable of justification, and potentially fallible."[34] To put it more simply, he tells us that engineering is really just an "ad hoc method of 'doing the best you can with what you've got.'"[35] The several dozen engineering heuristics discussed by Koen include rules of thumb for specific applications, but most have broad relevance. Examples of the latter include: "At some point in the project, freeze the design;"[36] "solve problems by successive approximations;"[37] and "work at the margin of solvable problems."[38]

Koen's main concern is to emphasize that while engineers will use whatever works to solve a problem, they also implicitly recognize the fallibility of their strategy—they are interminable doubters when it comes to assuming that a particular strategy is true for all times and places. Thus engineers have no illusions about mastering the natural world or possessing solutions to every problem, much less about controlling human history. Indeed, for all his effort to clarify what he means by heuristics, Koen only serves to highlight the complexity and messiness of engineering. Almost every heuristic requires an engineer to make significant judgments: they still have to determine *when* to freeze a design; they still have to determine *which* approximations are appropriate; and they still have to determine *where* the margins of a solvable problem lie. Most importantly, engineering designs are always being evaluated according to a moving target—the best practices or, as Koen likes to call them, the "state of the art," are in constant flux. For all the effort engineers expend trying to develop and propagate these best practices, as evident in libraries full of design handbooks, not to mention the myriad of regulatory policies and laws, engineers are only ever necessary to the extent that ambiguity and uncertainty are present in the design process.

What then can be said about what happens "on the margins" of a problem being addressed by an engineer? How are engineering judgments made? What can be said beyond the insistence of engineers such as Jack Swearengen that "design is not a purely objective and rational process"?[39] Vincenti argues that, in addition to varieties of explicit knowledge, "we must add the implicit, wordless, pictureless knowledge essential to engineering judgment . . . tacit knowledge."[40] The historian of technology Eugene Ferguson agrees, pointing out that "successful design still requires the stores of expert tacit knowledge and intuitive 'feel' of experience."[41] Thus: "No matter how vigorously a 'science' of design may be pushed, the successful design of real things in a contingent world will always be based more on art than on science. Unquantifiable judgments and choices are the elements that determine the way a design comes together."[42]

Underlining this point, the civil engineer Samuel C. Florman argues that "engineers agree that intuition, practical experience, and artistic sensibility are at least as important to their work as is the application of scientific theory."[43] Indeed, he insists that "although engineering is serious and methodical, it contains elements of spontaneity. Engineering is an art as well as a science, and good engineering depends upon leaps of imagination as well as painstaking care."[44]

These references to the artistic dimension of engineering design provide further clues to the kinds of things that influence engineering judgment in the midst of "leaps of imagination." Obvious examples include aesthetics and emotion, and this section will conclude with a brief discussion of the latter. As Florman puts it: "the fact that engineers are inarticulate[!] does not signify that engineering does not evoke strong emotions."[45] He goes on to say that "analysis, rationality, materialism, and practical creativity do not preclude emotional fulfillment; they are pathways to such fulfillment. They do not 'reduce' experience, they expand it."[46] Of course, the emotional side of engineering is also revealed by the fact that, for the most part, it is a collective, not an individual pursuit. Engineers do not face constraints imposed solely by the natural world, but constraints such as cost, time, and personality conflicts—all of which are subjective, and involve personal relationships. Aerospace engineer Louis Bucciarelli's study of three different engineering firms makes this point clearly: "the process of designing is a process of achieving consensus among participants with different 'interests' in the design. . . . [It] is necessarily social and requires the participants to negotiate their differences and construct meaning through direct, and preferably face-to-face, exchange."[47]

For this reason the philosopher Michael Davis suggests that although "engineers often describe themselves as applying natural science to practical problems, they could just as easily, and more accurately, describe themselves as applying knowledge of how people work in a certain industry."[48]

Engineering the Church, Properly Understood

What then do these insights into the practice of engineering mean for my portrayal of Yoder as a harsh critic of engineering who at the same time appeared to think like an engineer? What are the implications of labeling Yoder an engineer of the church? First, I would argue that the issues Yoder is confronting in his critique of engineering are valid, but misplaced, for good engineering does not exhibit the characteristics he thinks it does. Good engineering can be seen to counter, rather than elevate the problematic tendencies of Constantinianism that Yoder was so attuned to, in the sense that it is marked by heuristics and tacit skills rather than the drive for control and mastery. Engineering is more accurately thought of as a kind of artistry rather than the application of theoretical reasoning. Thus the practice of engineering is not, as Yoder suggests, diametrically opposed to his own understanding of the way the church should relate to the world. A concern for effectiveness that recognizes the subjectivity and the fallibility of the means utilized—which is what good engineering is really all about—may be able to work *with* rather than against God's purposes. In short, the practice of engineering provides a glimpse of one way the church may be able to move beyond the deep-rooted tension between calls for effectiveness and calls for faithfulness.

Second, I would argue that the characteristics of the practice of engineering can enrich Yoder's approach to the life of the church. In my view, when Yoder falls short as a theologian it is not because he is trying to engineer the church but because he is not a good enough engineer. To the extent that Yoder's posture of radical reform fails to do more than highlight the need for effective change in the church—stopping short of trying to flesh out how it may be possible to help produce, achieve, or bring about a desired end—it remains inadequate.

Traces of this critique can be found in other readings of Yoder. For example, Conrad Brunk has argued that Yoder's insistence that "the church must avoid the temptation to 'take charge' and 'engineer' society" is inadequate, because, "if the church is to establish an alternative moral community, then it must 'take charge' of its own institutions and 'engineer' them in certain ways."[49] And yet Brunk's own perspective seems inadequate, given that he is willing to accept and apply Yoder's skewed understanding of engineering directly to the church—thus he equates engineering the church with "taking charge" of it. Even if the church really was an institution like any other, we have seen that engineers would recognize the futility of this kind of grasping for control, if not mastery.

There is still an important insight in Brunk's critique, an insight that Michael Cartwright makes clear when he accuses Yoder of not having an adequate appreciation of the importance of Christian formation. As Cartwright puts it: "Yoder can explain what church looks like, when it happens, but he does not bother to describe how it comes into being over time."[50] As eloquent as he is when it comes to explaining the potential impact of the practices of the church on the watching world, Yoder does not talk about the way these same practices come to impact those who make up the church. And so my depiction of Yoder as an engineer of the church shines a spotlight on the need for further exploration into the way the practices of the church contribute to the formation of faithful witnesses to Christ. It compels further exploration into what makes something like, for example, Yoder's posture of radical reformation possible.[51]

To sum up, I do not think we should try to circumvent Yoder's concern to bring about effective change in the church. Nor do I think that we should be under any illusions that the moving of God's Spirit can be fully explained by an examination of the practices of the church. The key is that, just as good engineers are aware of their dependence on heuristics and tacit skills, good theologians—good engineers of the church—must acknowledge their own dependence on heuristics and tacit skills, proclaiming their trust that God is at work in ways they hardly imagine. What the church needs is doxology and engineering.

Notes

1. John Howard Yoder, *For the Nations: Essays Public and Evangelical* (Grand Rapids, MI: Eerdmans, 1997). All the essays included in this collection were previously presented and/or published elsewhere, and were arranged thematically, not chronologically.

2. Ibid., 201.

3. Ibid., 209.

4. Ibid., 210.

5. Ibid.

6. Ibid., 104.

7. Ibid., 108.

8. Ibid., 122.

9. Ibid., 81.

10. Ibid., 119.

11. John Howard Yoder, *The Priestly Kingdom: Social Ethics as Gospel* (Notre Dame, IN: University of Notre Dame Press, 1984), 140.

12. Ibid.

13. See "Paul Polak Project" file, box 196, John H. Yoder (1927-1997) Collection, Mennonite Church USA Archives, Goshen, IN.

14. Yoder, *For the Nations*, 150.

15. Ibid., 196.

16. Ibid., 216 (emphasis added).

17. Ibid., 218 (emphasis added).

18. Ibid., 118 (emphasis added).

19. John Howard Yoder, *The Christian Witness to the State* (Eugene, OR: Wipf & Stock, 1998), 19 (emphasis added).

20. Yoder, *For the Nations*, 119.

21. John Howard Yoder, *Body Politics: Five Practices of the Christian Community Before the Watching World* (Scottdale, PA: Herald Press, 2001).

22. Ibid., 11.

23. Yoder, *The Priestly Kingdom*, 5.

24. Ibid., 16.

25. John Howard Yoder, "Historiography as a Ministry to Renewal," in *From Faith to Age: Historians and the Modern Church: A Festschrift for Donald F. Durnbaugh*, ed. David B. Eller, *Brethren Life and Thought* 43, nos. 3 & 4 (1997): 217.

26. Yoder, *The Priestly Kingdom*, 5.

27. Ibid.

28. Yoder, "Historiography as a Ministry to Renewal," 217.

29. Yoder, *The Priestly Kingdom*, 69.

30. MacIntyre's fullest discussion of practices is found in *After Virtue: A Study in Moral Theory*, 2nd ed. (Notre Dame, IN: University of Notre Dame Press, 1984), 187.

31. Walter Vincenti, *What Engineers Know and How They Know It: Analytical Studies from Aeronautical History* (Baltimore: Johns Hopkins University Press, 1990), 6.

32. Henry Petroski, *Invention by Design: How Engineers Get From Thought to Thing* (Cambridge, MA: Harvard University Press, 1996), 141.

33. Billy Vauhn Koen, *Discussion of the Method: Conducting the Engineer's Approach to Problem Solving* (New York: Oxford University Press, 2003), 7.

34. Ibid., 28.

35. Ibid., 93.

36. Ibid., 35.

37. Ibid., 38.

38. Ibid., 72.

39. Jack Clayton Swearengen, *Beyond Paradise: Technology and the Kingdom of God: A Prophetic Primer for Church Leaders* (Eugene, OR: Wipf & Stock, 2007), 194. To be clear, Swearengen does not lament this state of affairs—he goes on to say that design "is not intended to be" objective, "and it cannot be."

40. Vincenti, *What Engineers Know and How They Know It*, 198.

41. Eugene Ferguson, *Engineering and the Mind's Eye* (Cambridge, MA: MIT Press, 1992), 171.

42. Ibid., 194.

43. Samuel C. Florman, "Subsumed by Science?" *Technology Review* 100, no. 3 (1997): 59.

44. Samuel C. Florman, *The Existential Pleasures of Engineering*, 2nd ed. (New York: St. Martin's Griffin, 1996), 182.

45. Ibid., 98.

46. Ibid., 101.

47. Louis Bucciarelli, *Designing Engineers* (Cambridge, MA: The MIT Press, 1994), 159.

48. Michael Davis, *Thinking Like an Engineer* (New York: Oxford University Press, 1990), 24.

49. Conrad Brunk, Review of *For the Nations* by John Howard Yoder, *Conrad Grebel Review* 16, no. 2 (1998): 131.

50. Michael G. Cartwright, "Sharing the House of God: Learning to Read Scripture with Anabaptists," *Mennonite Quarterly Review* 74, no. 4 (2000): 610.

51. This resonates with Gerald W. Schlabach's recent critique of Yoder's inability to recognize the extent to which his own posture of dissent was the result of his standing point within a "tradition of dissent." See "Continuity and Sacrament, or Not: Hauerwas, Yoder, and their Deep Difference," *Journal of the Society of Christian Ethics* 27, no. 2 (2007): 189.

Chapter 8

Universal History and a Not-Particularly Christian Particularity:
Jeremiah and John Howard Yoder's Social Gospel

Paul Martens

In recent years, a wide variety of claims have been expounded concerning the legacy of John Howard Yoder. On one side, there are some who have emphasized a pronounced emphasis on the unique life and death of Jesus as definitive for Christian theology and ethics.[1] On another side, it is beginning to appear that Yoder understood a certain expression of Christianity to be very similar to a certain expression of Judaism, pushing his ecumenical and sociological concerns against the absolute uniqueness of Christianity.[2] On a third side, secular thinkers have begun to appropriate aspects of the politics of Yoder without particular interest in the theological importance of either Jesus or Christianity.[3]

Recognizing these three positions (of the many that have been articulated), several questions present themselves to Yoder's readers: can all of these apparently contradictory appropriations really be rooted in Yoder's corpus? If so, how is this possible? And, if one believes that Yoder was "a man who seemed never to have changed his mind,"[4] or that "Yoder's writings and concerns display an amazing consistency from the 1950s to the 1990s,"[5] the problem of reconciling these divergent claims becomes more difficult.

In the following pages, I will sketch Yoder's gradual evolution from articulating a strong Jesus-centered ethic towards an articulation of a less-than-particularly Christian social ethic rooted in a construal of universal history, thereby providing an account of how there can be such a wide variety of appropriations of Yoder's thought. In doing so, I necessarily challenge the claim that Yoder's writings display an amazing consistency by tracing the subtle and substantial semantic shift from eschatology to doxology to worship in his understanding of a Christian's relationship to history.

As the subtitle indicates, a significant portion of my argument lies in Yoder's interpretation and use of the Old Testament prophet Jeremiah. In order to flesh out the issues involved in arguing that Yoder provides an account of universal history, I must begin by examining the foundational article of Reinhard Hütter, whose "The Church: Midwife of History or Witness of the Eschaton?"[6] presents a thesis directly challenging the one I make here. In the context of his argument, Hütter juxtaposes Yoder with Walter Rauschenbusch, thereby enabling Rauschenbusch to serve as a conversation partner in the background, occasionally helping to refocus our view of Yoder's conception of history throughout the rest of this essay.

The structure of my argument, therefore, leans heavily on Hütter's foundational work. To begin, I summarily sketch Hütter's articulation of the similarities and differences between Rauschenbusch and Yoder. In light of Hütter's claims, I introduce the role that Jeremiah plays in this conversation as a way of: (a) expanding Hütter's range to include reference to Yoder's work beyond his *The Politics of Jesus* (1972); (b) forcing us to recognize a significant shift in Yoder's language vis-à-vis history from eschatology to doxology to worship as instrumentality; and on these bases, (c) challenging the consistency of Hütter's claims concerning Yoder, and thereby the supposed "fundamental difference" between Yoder and Rauschenbusch.

Examining Hütter's Yoder

In "The Church: Midwife of History or Witness of the Eschaton?" Reinhard Hütter argues that Yoder and Rauschenbusch represent "two alternative 'paradigms' of ecclesiologically centered thought in Christian social ethics." To make this argument interesting, he outlines the similarities first: (1) both understand Jesus as normative for social ethics; (2) both represent Jesus' death as a political death, as a political threat to the Establishment; (3) both understand the cross as the final expression of Jesus' life, a revelation of Jesus' nonresistance; (4) both understand the church as the historical continuation of the life and death of Jesus; (5)

both understand the church as "the heuristic location from whence God's acting in the world can be perceived"; (6) both attribute a similar "aggressivity" to the church in its mission; (7) both hold the church to be of an inherently ethical nature.[7]

Drawn in this fashion, the similarities are surprising, as Hütter himself acknowledges; drawn clearly in this fashion, it is surprising that nearly all of the scholarly attention to Yoder's theological forerunners has been paid to Barth (positively) and the Niebuhrs (negatively).

But Hütter is not interested in concluding that Yoder and Rauschenbusch say the same thing, as the questioning either/or in his subtitle indicates: "Midwife of History or Witness of the Eschaton?" Rather, the central point in comparing the two is to show that they are, in fact, fundamentally different. I will begin by citing the fundamental difference and then work back to Hütter's construal of the logic supporting the difference. Hütter states the difference as follows:

> We are thus able finally to discern the fundamental difference that sets Rauschenbusch and Yoder at odds despite all their similarities. Rauschenbusch understands *history as universal eschatology* whereas Yoder understands *eschatology as particular history*. Their respective ecclesiologies reflect this basic divergence, and it shapes the unfolding of their ecclesial ethics.[8]

In this context, I will tentatively accept and turn away from Hutter's account of Rauschenbusch in order to attend more fully to his claims concerning Yoder. First, for Yoder, Hütter argues that both of the terms *history* and *eschatology* are dependent upon the prior notion of the church as the community that prefigures the "kingdom of God." What this means is that for Yoder, "history" has no meaning in and of itself, no purpose, no inner logic. Rather, history is merely the framework within which the church evangelizes.[9] Contrary to the familiar trope—the church is responsible for the course of history—Yoder posits the opposite: eschatology turns into history, meaning that true history only comes into existence as the eschaton enters history through the life of the church. To clarify, Hütter states: "In this very transparency the eschaton enters history and 'makes history' in the history of its own prefiguration in the church."[10]

As good as this sounds, I count three uses of the term *history* in this one sentence. Let me pause briefly to try to separate these three definitions as employed by Hütter: (1) the eschaton enters history—or the mere meaningless framework of events in which Jesus through the church makes meaning; (2) the eschaton makes history—or the meaningful, purpose-filled existence that is eschatologically defined with reference to God's work; (3) the history of the prefiguration of the eschaton in the church—or the simple events of the life of the church that prefigure and instantiate the eschaton. It is obvious that the second and third uses are similar and qualitatively different from the first. I will return to this discussion shortly.

To revisit his concluding claims (universal versus particular), however, Hütter states that for Yoder, the church is *not* called to be a midwife helping to give birth to God's final rule in creation and to bring history (second use?) to its fulfillment. Rather, the church is simply called to be *transparent* in its existence as the community that witnesses to the character of God's love as it was revealed in Jesus of Nazareth.[11] And it is important to note that the one and decisive criterion for Yoder's specific kind of involvement is to be found in the cross. More specifically, Hütter goes on to state: "the message is *to be found nowhere else* than in its representative medium: first in the life and death of Jesus, then and now in the witness of the church as the 'new social order.'"[12]

The Challenge of Yoder's Jeremiah

Near the beginning of this essay, I made the cryptic comment that one of my intentions is to push Hütter's version of Yoder beyond the boundaries set by *The Politics of Jesus*, published first in 1972. For Hütter, as for many others, this text is central, and several even earlier texts (four, to be precise)[13] are cited to support the identification of Yoder with *The Politics of Jesus*. The only exception to this rule in Hütter's article are rare references to *The Priestly Kingdom*, published later in 1984.[14]

For readers of these early texts, there are probably few disagreements with Hütter's portrayal of Yoder's position, with its strong account of the church, the centrality of the cross, and the idiosyncrasy of the message spoken and lived by Jesus. But when examining some of Yoder's later texts, a few of these strong claims become equivocal. To illustrate my claim, allow me to introduce three of Yoder's familiar texts—texts published in at least two venues—as representative snapshots of the increasing equivocation: (1) "Peace Without Eschatology?" (1954); (2) "To Serve Our God and to Rule the World" (1988); and (3) "See How They

Go with Their Face to the Sun" (1995). In examining this development, I will utilize the increasing importance of Jeremiah to illuminate precisely why and how Yoder's claims concerning Jeremiah's Judaism ultimately challenge Hütter's construal of the uniqueness of the cross, the church, and the dismissal of history outside the particularity of the church.

1. *"Peace Without Eschatology?"* The little article known as "Peace Without Eschatology?" has appeared numerous times in collections of Yoder's works. Initially, it was a paper presented in 1954 at a theological study conference in the Netherlands, and later, it appeared in print in several venues, including a *Concern* pamphlet (1959), as "If Christ is Truly Lord" in *The Original Revolution* (1971), and more recently in *The Royal Priesthood* (1994). The frequent reprints can lead one to believe that the arguments contained in "Peace Without Eschatology?" are representative of the entirety of Yoder's thinking. But a closer look at the text reveals that this text reflects a very early stage in Yoder's thinking.

The purpose of "Peace Without Eschatology?" is to outline precisely how history and human endeavor can only be recognized and understood in the broader context of God's plan. In short, it is a pamphlet attempting to provide a rudimentary theological context for understanding how Christian discipleship and pacifism can make sense, to provide a rudimentary revised account of what is "real." On the surface, Yoder's definition of eschatology is simple: "a hope which, defying present frustration, defines a present position in terms of the yet unseen goal which gives it meaning."[15] That yet unseen goal is the eschaton, the last things, the ultimate divine certainty of "peace."

The critique implicit in this definition is, of course, directed against attempts to build peace without eschatology, or more accurately, with "wrong understandings of eschatology."[16] Against assumptions that peace can only be brought into history through force or political machination, Yoder argues that the incarnation and entire work of Christ decisively changed history, bringing peace through weakness and divine patience. In short, Christ inaugurated a "new aeon:"[17]

> The new aeon came into history in a decisive way with the incarnation and entire work of Christ. Christ had been awaited eagerly by Judaism for centuries; but when he came he was rejected, for the new aeon He revealed was not what men wanted. . . . The new aeon involves a radical break with the old.[18]

The point is clear: Christ is unique and the life and death of Jesus is the beginning of something new. The life and death of Christ understood in this way illuminates *agape*: love "that is willing to suffer any loss or seeming defeat for the sake of obedience"; love performed in such a way that "effectiveness and success had been sacrificed for the sake of love."[19] But prefiguring the argument more fully developed in *The Politics of Jesus*,[20] this sacrifice is and will be turned by God into victory. This is *"the only* valid starting point for Christian pacifism or nonresistance."[21]

Yoder goes on to claim, affirming Hütter's position, that the new aeon, revealed in Christ, does not alter the old aeon. Rather, the new aeon takes primacy over the old, proclaims the doom of the old, and begins to vanquish the old. In this sense, Christ inaugurates a new eschatological history alongside the preexisting forceful reign of the state over evil, vengeance, and chaos, which will eventually be overcome.[22]

From these preliminary observations, it is clear that Hütter's claims resonate with and are rooted in the perspective of this early text. If Hütter interpretively steps beyond the text at points, he does so in such a way that the spirit of the text is not violated. But there is one point of equivocation in "Peace Without Eschatology?" that I want to raise that serves as the bridge to the later texts I address below. The point of equivocation is found in the Old Testament prophet. At various points in the text the ambivalent role of the prophet forces its way between the either/or of the new and old aeons. For example, Yoder states the following:

> In the Old Testament the prophets had been lonely men, cut off from their people by their loyalty to God (which was, in the deepest sense, their real loyalty to their people, even though the people condemned them as troublemakers). Then in the New Testament the body of Christ came into being, a new people in the prophets' line, replacing disobedient Israel as the people of promise.[23]

Jeremiah is cited as one of these prophets, and little is said about him, except that he provided the corrective to the nationalistic turn in Judaism by proclaiming peace when there was no peace, by proclaiming peace without judgment, by proclaiming peace with eschatology.[24] That being said, precisely what it means to be in the prophets' line is merely intimated in "Peace Without Eschatology?" This idea becomes more pronounced years later, and to illustrate this ascendancy, allow me to turn to an examination of "To Serve Our God and to Rule the World." In this later text, the particular prophet of Jeremiah reemerges alongside a reconceived account of how to view history doxologically.

2. *"To Serve Our God and to Rule the World."* In 1988, John Howard Yoder provided the presidential address at the annual meeting of the Society of Christian Ethics and the published version appeared that same year as "To Serve Our God and to Rule the World."[25] Six years later, the same text also appeared in *The Royal Priesthood.*[26]

On the surface, "To Serve Our God and to Rule the World" appears to follow in the eschatological strain of "Peace Without Eschatology?" The text begins and ends with citations from the fifth chapter of John's Revelation, yet the language of eschatology used so carefully in "Peace Without Eschatology?" is notoriously absent in 1988. Rather, a refocusing on "reading history doxologically" has taken its place.

According to the later text, doxology is: "a mark of faith, is more than liturgy. It is a way of seeing; a grasp of which end is up, which way is forward."[27] Implicitly and explicitly, Yoder is critiquing what he takes to be a narrow understanding of doxology as simply liturgy, and he is expanding the definition of doxology to describe how one views one's "cosmic commitments," to describe how—like "Peace Without Eschatology?"—one views what is "real."[28] And, in this later text, the cosmic context is sketched from the biblical referents found in Revelation 5:7-14.

Despite this apparent similarity between the texts, things are not exactly what they seem. As Yoder begins to articulate what it means to see history doxologically, a reshaped assumption begins to make its presence felt, a reshaped assumption that shifts from attention to the eschaton as something in the future toward attention to Jesus' lordship in the present. In "Peace Without Eschatology?" Yoder argued for a view of reality that "defines a present position in terms of the yet unseen goal which gives it meaning,"[29] and for this reason, "peace" was not something that described external results of one's behavior but the character and goal of one's action performed with confidence in divine sovereignty. "To Serve Our God and to Rule the World," however, moves toward addressing external results of behavior, and seeing that "reality" now entails the demand that one is "obligated to discern, down through the centuries, which historical developments can be welcomed as progress in the light of the Rule of the Lamb."[30] In short, the shift is away from seeing the rise of the new aeon (a term also dropped in the later texts) in the church or the body of Christ[31] toward the progress of world history in light of the "Rule of the Lamb," of affirming and aligning oneself with the kingdom building behavior and morality of the good news.[32] To specify, Yoder states, "To see history doxologically is to appropriate as did Jesus the full and patent ambivalence of the Jewish experience with the usability of majesty, whether Canaanite kingdoms or Mesopotamian empires, as instruments of divine rule."[33] In place of the sharp break between Jesus and Judaism is ambivalent appropriation.

To address this appropriation, Yoder outlines some of the initial difficulties of the judges and kings in Israel, arguing that as long as the royal house of Judah stood, the strain of royal ideology of the Old Testament could claim equal status as the prophetic one. But in the early sixth century, "things began to be sorted out."[34] And the key figure in this "sorting out" in the Old Testament is Jeremiah. Yoder explains: "The age of Jeremiah, and his message, precipitated the definition of diaspora as not merely a chastisement but also a calling. To 'seek the peace of the city where JHWH has sent you' meant for Jewry all the way from Jeremiah to Rosenzweig and Bucer [*sic*] the acceptance of a non-sovereign, non-territorial self definition."[35]

Yoder then goes on to say that the rabbis after Jeremiah read history as "God's having ratified his word to Jeremiah."[36] In this respect, there was nothing different about the political stance of Jesus in the Gospels. In fact, in this text, Yoder sees only two differences between Jews and Christians: (1) Christians included Gentiles (not addressed in this context); and (2) Christians understood that the world is in the process of being brought under control by the Lamb (the focus of this context). But, concretely, to rule the world in fellowship with the Lamb always begins as a sociological and political statement:

> To "rule the world" in fellowship with the living Lamb will sometimes mean humbly building a grassroots culture, with Jeremiah. Sometimes (as with Joseph and Daniel) it will mean helping the pagan king solve one problem at a time. Sometimes (again as with Daniel and his friends) it will mean disobeying the King's imperative of idolatry, refusing to be bamboozled by the claims made for the Emperor's new robe or his finery.[37]

Certainly, vestiges of Yoder's earlier position dot the text, appearing as claims that "moral validation is derived from the imminent Kingdom which Jesus announces"[38] and that the image of the slaughtered Lamb "is the code reference" to Jesus, who serves as the criterion for discerning the meaning of particular events within history.[39] But clearly the shift from the non-empirical, reality-defining eschaton (finding the meaning of the future for the present) to doxology as discerning reality in the empirical past and present (finding meaning in the past and present) has subtly altered Yoder's articulation of a Christian's understanding of history.

3. *"See How They Go with Their Face to the Sun."* As I have already indicated, Jeremiah appears in several of Yoder's texts, but the central and eventually defining text that emerges late in his corpus is "See How They Go with Their Face to the Sun," first presented in 1995 and published in *For the Nations* (1997) and in *The Jewish-Christian Schism Revisited* (2003). In this later text, Yoder engages and builds upon Stephen Zweig's poem-drama *Jeremiah*. His central point, reiterating some of what he had already spelled out in "To Serve Our God and to Rule the World," is to demonstrate that Jeremiah already provides us with the necessary social perspective on how we should see our task and how Christians should act in the world: dispersion is our mission and vocation.[40]

Unlike the use of Jeremiah 6:13-15 and 8:7-14 in "Peace Without Eschatology?" the key text referred to in all of the late appearances of Jeremiah is found in 29:7: "seek the welfare of the city where I have sent you into exile, and pray to the LORD on its behalf, for in its welfare you will find your welfare." Against the ambiguous aims of the Davidic (Constantinian) project, Jeremiah's exhortation becomes the key to understanding "true" Judaism, the Judaism that opens the way for Yoder's Christianity.

In the course of the argument of "See How They Go with Their Face to the Sun," Yoder acknowledges that although he first expressed "Jewish quietism since Jeremiah" in sociological terms,[41] he continues: "Yet if you had asked those Jews (including the first Christians) to explain themselves and their attitude toward pagan empires . . . their answers would have been theological."

According to Yoder, they would have said: (1) that God is sovereign over history, and there is no need for them to seize or subvert political sovereignty for God's will to be done; (2) that establishing the ultimate righteous social order among nations will be the mission of the messiah and should be left to him; (3) that the failed message of the Maccabees, Zealots, etc., to restore national kingship has taught them a lessen; (4)

that if an all-righteous God wanted to chastise us for our sins, self-defense would interfere with God's purpose; (5) that the death of the righteous sanctifies the name of God.[42] On the basis of these answers, Yoder claims: "It is rather the case that Jesus' impact in the first century added more and deeper authentically Jewish reasons, and reinforced and further validated the already expressed Jewish reasons for the already well established ethos of not being in charge and not considering any local state structure to be the primary bearer of the movement of history."[43]

To look back on an earlier text of Yoder's not addressed above, this is an even stronger claim than that offered in "If Abraham is Our Father" (1971)—which ties the calling of Abraham to the gospel—that defines the original gospel revolution as a social revolution, as "the creation of a distinct community with its own deviant set of values and its coherent way of incarnating them."[44]

And continuing his argument with a self-conscious reference to "Peace Without Eschatology?" in the footnote, Yoder states, "To this same stance [Jesus' impact on the first century] the second generation of witnesses after Jesus, the 'apostles,' added another layer of further reasons, still utterly Jewish in form and substance, having to do with the messiahship of Jesus, his lordship, and the presence of the Spirit."[45]

Whether Yoder is right or wrong is not the issue here, but this claim is certainly not what Yoder says in "Peace Without Eschatology?" where Jesus "proclaimed the institution of a new kind of life."[46] The late Yoder has ecumenically attempted to bring Judaism and Christianity together in both their sociological expression of "not being in charge" and in their theological reasons for doing so. But in the process, he has reduced many of his earlier claims to secondary afterthoughts, if not untruths; claims that the life and death of Jesus is uniquely definitional, claims that peace is a goal and hope but not observable results of behavior, claims that Jeremiah proclaimed "peace" when there was no peace are all reframed and subordinated to the ongoing privileged position of "not being in charge," and it is precisely this subordination of particularly Christian theological claims to their verification in the progress of history that allows Yoder to affirm Tolstoy's claim: "progress in history is borne by the underdogs,"[47] a claim that, according to Yoder, can be verified by "serious social science."[48]

Commenting further on precisely what it means to "seek the peace of the city," Yoder states:

"Seek the peace of the city" is too weak a translation for Jeremiah's command. It should be translated "seek the salvation of the culture to which God has sent you." Joseph's answer to Egypt's famine problem, or Daniel's role in Darius' reorganization of the Persian empire into manageable satrapies, represents proto-typically a Jewish role in contributing to secular well-being which is far more than mere minority survival.[49]

And here, the issue is starkly revealed: "peace" becomes synonymous with "the salvation of the culture" in social and political terms, and "secular well-being" is Yoder's own phrase. The underdog, the minority, and the oppressed are the bearers of historical progress, of the salvation of culture, of the ethos of not being in charge. But, is this the "age of the church" spoken of so eloquently in "Peace Without Eschatology?"

The Church, Worship, and Yoder's Social Gospel

In sketching the fundamental difference between Yoder and Rauschenbusch, Hütter argues that their respective ecclesiologies reflect their understanding of history. This link is very important, and for this reason I have begun to illuminate the link between Yoder's shifting view of history and how this plays itself out in ecclesiology.

In 1982, in "The Hermeneutics of Peoplehood," Yoder defined worship as "the communal cultivation of an alternative construction of society and history."[50] But, as one can see by the paradigmatic role assigned to Jeremiah in the later writings, the concern for building an alternative community apart from the world has been virtually abandoned. Yes, the church is part of an alternative construction of society and history, but the church is no longer solely responsible for defining the new age, for bearing witness to the new aeon inaugurated by Christ. Rather, the church is assigned a role in discerning and bringing about the history borne by the underdog, the oppressed, the minority or, in short, it is assigned to "seek the peace of the city." Therefore, one should not be surprised to find that Yoder refers to the church as serving instrumentally in the renewal of the world in *Body Politics*.[51] Yoder's anti-sectarian emphasis finally reaches its zenith in these later works, where the work of the church becomes defined through a reinterpretation of the sacraments, the social processes that are inaugurated for the purposes of bringing about the renewal of the world.[52]

Returning to the beginning, to Hütter's differentiation between particular and universal history, I suggest that Yoder does have an account of universal history, or at least an account of a particular history (that borne by the underdog, etc.) in service of a universal history. And granting that Hütter may be right about the early Yoder, I would argue that the late Yoder does not have an account of history as eschatological (as Yoder himself drops the term) unless he means an increasingly realized or immanent eschatology. In the late Yoder, the sacraments become the instruments of service; the sacraments become social processes that are "phenomenon in and for 'the real world.'"[53] And in the face of several possible objections, Yoder rhetorically asks: "Why should it not be the case that God's purpose for the world would pursue an organic logic through history and across the agenda of the pilgrim people's social existence with such a reliable rhythm as we have here observed?"[54]

Notice what is said: organic logic through history, pilgrim people, reliable rhythm, what can be observed. Notice what is absent in this question: reference to Jesus? Christianity? the church? The key is a pilgrim people's social existence, the original gospel revolution, whether they be Christian or not. Or to restate, "that the oppressed are the bearers of the meaning of history is not poetry but serious social science."[55] And with this observation we can read the allegedly Barthian claim made at the beginning of *For the Nations* with a new set of sociologically and politically focused eyes:

> The calling of the people of God is thus no different from the calling of all humanity. The difference between the human community as a whole ("*Bürgergemeinde*") and the faith community ("*Christengemeinde*") is a matter of awareness or knowledge or commitment or celebration, but not ultimate destiny.

What believers are called to is no different from what all humanity is called to.[56]

But unlike Barth's insistence that the faith community be called and defined by Christ, Yoder's late social gospel takes a problematic shape. In subordinating Christian theological particularity to sociological particularity, what remains are the social processes in service of the universal *telos* of humanity (with the Christian particularity optional). The church is no longer merely a witness, as Hütter would have it. Rather, much like Rauschenbusch, the church is a midwife for a new humanity and the instrument for bringing history to fulfillment. And the instrumentality of the church is not necessarily unique. In concluding "See How They Go with Their Face to the Sun," Yoder exemplifies the limits of the Jewish-Christian trajectory that he has attempted to unify in addressing the challenges in the face of bringing history to fulfillment. He states:

> I close by declaring my complete lack of authority to answer this next question. Is there something about this Jewish vision of the dignity and ministry of the scattered people of God which might be echoed or replicated by other migrant peoples, like the expatriate Chinese around the edge of Asia or the Indians in East and South Africa? Might it give hope to other refugees, the Armenians who were scattered in the 1920's? To other victims of imperial displacement, like African Americans? To the victims of the most recent horrors of Rwanda or the Balkans?[57]

Framing the question in this way makes sense only if the goal is to challenge imperialism, Constantinianism, and the strain of history synonymous with the apparently divinely sanctioned conquest of Canaan. In short, it only makes sense on the assumption that no one but the underdog bears the meaning of history. And this not-particularly Christian particular issue is the concern of many people. It should not surprise anyone, then, that Yoder is appropriated by secular thinkers wishing to make precisely the same political argument. Certainly in his later years, Yoder seems to encourage this appropriation with his apparent reduction of Christianity to a socio-political posture.

Is this the "real" Yoder? Perhaps that is a question that can be left open indefinitely. What I have attempted to illuminate is the reality that there are several faces of and phases in Yoder's corpus, and although these different elements may seem to say the same thing on the surface, subtle and substantial semantic shifts occur through the corpus that signal a vibrant, ever-engaged thinker who is continually growing into new conceptualizations and construals of the practices of the church. In this way, I would agree with Mark Thiessen Nation that Yoder is consistent. But in terms of content, I hope the above is sufficient to demonstrate that Yoder does, in fact, change his mind.

Notes

1. One could include both Craig Carter's *The Politics of the Cross: The Theology and Social Ethics of John Howard Yoder* (Grand Rapids, MI: Brazos Press, 2001) and Mark Thiessen Nation's *John Howard Yoder: Mennonite Patience, Evangelical Witness, Catholic Convictions* (Grand Rapids, MI: Eerdmans, 2006) in this group, alongside the Yoder usually appropriated by Stanley Hauerwas as evidenced, for example, in *A Better Hope: Resources for a Church Confronting Capitalism, Democracy, and Postmodernity* (Grand Rapids, MI: Brazos, 2000), 129-36.

2. See, for example, the comments made by Michael Cartwright and Peter Ochs in *The Jewish-Christian Schism Revisited* (Grand Rapids, MI: Eerdmans, 2003) and A. James Reimer's "Theological Orthodoxy and Jewish Christianity: A Personal Tribute to John Howard Yoder," in *The Wisdom of the Cross: Essays in Honor of John Howard Yoder*, ed. Stanley Hauerwas, et al, (Grand Rapids, MI: Eerdmans, 1999), 430-48.

3. See, for example, Romand Coles' "The Wild Patience of John Howard Yoder: 'Outsiders' and the 'Otherness of the Church,'" *Modern Theology* 18, no. 3 (2002): 305-31.

4. A. James Reimer, "Mennonites, Christ, and Culture: The Yoder Legacy," *Conrad Grebel Review* 16, no. 2 (1998): 6.

5. Nation, *John Howard Yoder*, 75.

6. Reinhard Hütter, "The Church: Midwife of History or Witness of the Eschaton?" *Journal of Religious Ethics* 18, no. 1 (1990): 27-54.

7. Ibid., 40-45.

8. Ibid., 47.

9. Ibid., 46.

10. Ibid., 48.

11. Ibid., 48.

12. Ibid., 44 (emphasis added).

13. The four explicitly referred to by Hütter are: "The Otherness of the Church" (1961); *The Christian Witness to the State* (1964); "A People in the World" (1969); and *The Original Revolution* (1971).

14. See John Howard Yoder, *The Priestly Kingdom: Social Ethics as Gospel* (Notre Dame, IN: University of Notre Dame, 1984). Hütter notes this text twice in the text, on 44-45, and on 52 n5.

15. John Howard Yoder, *The Original Revolution: Essays on Christian Pacifism* (1971; repr. Scottdale, PA: Herald Press, 2003), 53.

16. Ibid., 54.

17. Ibid., 55-56.

18. Ibid., 55.

19. Ibid., 56-57.

20. See Chapter 12, "The War of the Lamb," in Yoder's *The Politics of Jesus*, 2nd ed (Grand Rapids, MI: Eerdmans, 1994), 226-47.

21. Yoder, *Original Revolution*, 56 (emphasis added).

22. Ibid., 58-59.

23. Ibid., 58.

24. Yoder, *Original Revolution*, 64-65. See Jeremiah 6:13-15 and 8:7-14.

25. John Howard Yoder, "To Serve Our God and to Rule the World," *The Annual for the Society of Christian Ethics* (1988): 3-14.

26. John Howard Yoder, *The Royal Priesthood: Essays Ecclesiological and Ecumenical*, ed. Michael G. Cartwright (Scottdale, PA: Herald Press, 1998), 128-40.

27. Ibid., 129.

28. Ibid., 129.

29. Yoder, *Original Revolution*, 53.

30. Yoder, *Royal Priesthood*, 132.

31. Yoder, *Original Revolution*, 55.

32. Yoder, *Royal Priesthood*, 136.

33. Ibid., 133.

34. Ibid.

35. Yoder, *Royal Priesthood*, 133. It appears that Bucer should be replaced with Buber (see *The Jewish-Christian Schism Revisited* [Grand Rapids, MI: Eerdmans, 2003], 85-86, where Rosenzweig and Buber are tied together in this same lineage).

36. Yoder, *Royal Priesthood*, 134.

37. Ibid., 135.

38. Ibid., 136.

39. Ibid., 132-33.

40. John Howard Yoder, *For the Nations: Essays Public and Evangelical* (Grand Rapids, MI: Eerdmans, 1997), 52.

41. Ibid., 67.

42. Ibid., 67-68.

43. Ibid., 69.

44. Yoder, *Original Revolution*, 28.

45. Yoder, *For the Nations*, 69.

46. Yoder, *Original Revolution*, 55.

47. Yoder, *Royal Priesthood*, 137.

48. Yoder, *For the Nations*, 35.

49. Yoder, *For the Nations*, 76 n60.

50. John Howard Yoder, "The Hermeneutics of Peoplehood: A Protestant Perspective on Practical Moral Reasoning," *Journal of Religious Ethics* 10, no.1 (1982): 64.

51. John Howard Yoder, *Body Politics: Five Practices of the Christian Community Before the Watching World* (Scottdale, PA: Herald Press, 2001), 78.

52. See Paul Martens, "The Problematic Development of the Sacraments in the Thought of John Howard Yoder," *Conrad Grebel Review* 24, no. 3 (2006): 65-77.

53. Yoder, *Body Politics*, x.

54. Ibid., 80.

55. Yoder, *For the Nations*, 35. In fact, this sentiment is already expressed in "To Serve Our God to Rule the World" (*Royal Priesthood*, 137).

56. Yoder, *For the Nations*, 24.

57. Yoder, *For the Nations*, 78.

Chapter 9

Unbinding Yoder from Just Policing

Andy Alexis-Baker

In recent years, some of the most influential Christian ethicists have actively reflected on the place of policing in North American peace theology. With the goal of replacing warfare with "policing," these ethicists are attempting to develop a theology of security in order to provide guidance for policy advocates and makers, and some of them believe such a theology could heal church divisions over pacifism. In an effort to bolster their position, many of these scholars have cited sections of John Howard Yoder's works in which he distinguished between policing and war.

Contributors to *Sojourners Magazine* have repeatedly invoked Yoder's name to support their arguments for international policing. Jim Wallis, *Sojourners'* editor, claimed:

> It is time to explore a theology for global police forces, including ethics for the use of internationally sanctioned enforcement—precisely as an alternative to war. Mennonite theologian John Howard Yoder was engaged in that very task near the end of his life. He was asking whether those committed to nonviolence might support the kind of necessary force utilized by police, because it is (or is designed to be) much more constrained, controlled, and circumscribed by the rule of law than is the violence of war, which knows few real boundaries. If that is true for the function of domestic police, how might it be extrapolated to an international police force acting with the multinational authorization of international law? Yoder's work in this area was never completed, but perhaps now it should be.[1]

Gerald Schlabach, who has developed a theory he calls "just policing," has referenced Yoder numerous times.[2] Echoing Wallis, Schlabach has stated that Yoder "was noting the difference [between war and policing] more and more regularly in the latter years of his career" and cited *The Politics of Jesus* as an example.[3] In *Kingdom Ethics*, Glen Stassen and David Gushee contended that "discipleship-pacifists," who see nonviolence as a way of life, are "slightly more flexible than rule-pacifists," who see nonviolence as a rule to follow. They cited Bonhoeffer's support of a plot to kill Hitler and Yoder's distinction between war and policing as examples of that flexibility.[4] Finally, in his 2008 book, *Peace: A History of Movements and Ideas*, ethicist David Cortright argues that "absolute pacifism" is an alienating, inflexible minority position. Instead, he argues for "pragmatic pacifism," which entails a "continuum of perspectives ranging from rejection of military violence and extending across a range of options that allow for some limited use of force under specific circumstances."[5] He then cites John Howard Yoder's distinction between war and policing as an example of a pacifist who could accept "multilateral peace operations to protect civilian populations."[6] Furthermore, Cortright claims that pragmatic pacifism is a combination of pacifism and the just war theory and that John Howard Yoder supported such a position.[7]

Despite a variety of motives, these authors define Yoder's legacy in ways that echo the justifiable war tradition instead of his own Messianic pacifist position. Yet no one has systematically examined passages in Yoder's writings that pertain to policing. In this article, I will review Yoder's key passages on policing and argue that any use of his work to rally Christians behind "just policing" does not befit his legacy. Yoder never intended to develop "a theology for global police forces." These scholars have misread Yoder because of their narrow focus on questions on the police's minimal use of violence. Subsequently, they have also failed to appreciate that even nonviolence can be an oppressive tactic when the police use it.[8]

Policing and Totalitarianism

In *The Christian Witness to the State*, published in 1964,[9] Yoder differentiated a "crusade concept" of war from a "police conception of limited war . . . guided by fair judicial processes, subject to recognized legislative regulation, and safeguarded in practice against its running away with the situation. Only the absolute minimum of violence is therefore in any way excusable."[10] Although the state's police function is "not intrinsically legitimate,"[11] Christians could use it to call state officials to "eliminate specific visible abuses." Nevertheless, Christians should be wary of the state's police function because the state continually uses it to try and create an idealized society: "Instead of seeing itself as the guardian of the stability of a 'tolerable balance of egoisms' . . . the policeman or statesman comes to consider himself as being responsible for bringing into existence an ideal order."[12] This attempt will "always be less successful than hoped" because elites impose their ideals on their subjects and glorify themselves. The police function, therefore, can help to temper violence, but simultaneously creates—through bureaucracy or brute force—new oppressions.

Because state policing tends to generate new opportunities for oppression, Yoder expressed serious doubts about a "one central world government with unchallengeable coercive powers" embodied in an international police force. Instead, he argued, "true international unity will grow best through the imponderable contributions of labor, food, health, postal, and other such collaboration where the sanctions of police violence are not constantly just below the surface."[13] Thus Yoder did not use the state's police function as a theoretical foundation for creating a stronger state or international system.

Mindful of this skepticism, we can interpret his comment that, "The policing function of the state is to a degree legitimate and . . . war is illegitimate, for the clear reason that the police function can fit the prescriptions of Romans 13 and 1 Timothy 2; it can distinguish the innocent from the guilty and can preserve a semblance of order."[14] Yet "legitimate," he further qualified, does not mean "good":

> In the relevant alternatives which we hold before men of state to give body to our critique, none will be good in the Christian sense; they will only be less evil. The term legitimate expresses this kind of qualified acquiescence according to the less wrong. When, for instance, we say . . . that police activity is legitimate and war is illegitimate, even for nations legitimate does not mean right and good; it points rather to the minimal level of wrong (i.e., of disconformity to Christ, our only standard of right and good) which is the best we can expect under the circumstances.[15]

For Yoder then, policing could serve as a conceptual critique of the war system, but Christians should not idolize the concept as a good or mislabel it as "peacemaking," as some scholars have recently done.[16] For Yoder, policing under the nation-state remains an evil to which God has not called Christians to participate.

Policing and Romans 13

In *The Politics of Jesus*, published in 1972, Yoder methodically rebutted mainstream Protestant readings of Romans 13, which assert that Christians have a moral duty to support and participate in state killing by virtue of the state's divine mandate to wield the sword. First, Yoder claimed that Romans 13 is lodged within the New Testament's wider view of the state as a demonic power.[17] This broader view sets the context of Romans, in which Paul exhorts Christians to love their enemies (chapter 12) and identifies the Roman government as an enemy to bear with nonresistantly (chapter 13). Though the government exercises vengeance that belongs to God (13:4), Christians must refuse to take vengeance (12:19). "This makes clear that the function exercised by government is not the function to be exercised by Christians," Yoder writes.[18] The "function" Paul forbade Christians to participate in was not only war but more importantly "police service."[19] Thus Yoder's brief comments on policing in *The Politics of Jesus* are set within a broader argument that the state is a conquered enemy that exercises a vengeance prohibited to Christians.

Though Christians are forbidden to participate in policing, the difference between war and policing is structurally significant. Police direct their violence toward the offender alone; the police are subject to inquiry from a higher authority; and the police only employ enough violence to subdue the offender. War, on the other hand, kills on a massive and indiscriminate scale that has little regulation. Based on this interpretation, Yoder claimed that Romans 13 does not give the state a blank check to wage war but sets limits upon state violence, perhaps similar to just war criteria. But this is not a positive recommendation: "The doctrine of the 'just war' is an effort to extend into the realm of war the logic of the limited violence of police authority—but not a very successful one. There is some logic to the 'just war' pattern of thought but very little realism."[20] Policing remains violent and has failed to meaningfully limit war thus far.

Ironically, when scholars use this passage from *The Politics of Jesus* to support police violence, they take it out of context in the same way that mainstream Protestants have taken Romans 13 out of its context. But Yoder's words about Romans 13 apply equally to his own book: "The call is to a nonresistant attitude toward a tyrannical government. This is the immediate and concrete meaning of the text; how strange then to make it the classic proof for the duty of Christians to kill."[21]

Policing and Yoder's Historical Narrative

Although Yoder differentiated between war and policing in several other writings, he used this distinction most frequently in *Christian Attitudes to War, Peace and Revolution.* Yoder narrated early Christian acceptance of policing as an aspect of "creeping Empire loyalty." Though Tertullian denounced Christians being part of the military, from 170 CE a few Christians were enlisted as soldiers, functioning, Yoder noted, mostly as bureaucrats: "They carried the mail, administered roads, and enforced the laws and the prison system."[22] As long as the soldiers did not kill or worship false gods, the church quietly decided to allow them to remain. This acquiescence to policing took a decisive turn at the Council of Arles in 314, when church leaders instructed even bureaucratic soldiers to remain in the military.[23] This allowed Ambrose and Augustine, in the late fourth century, to signal a "fundamentally new political ethic" for Christians that did not make love for enemies central: Christians could now kill enemies in loyalty to the Empire.[24] In his telling of early Christian history, Yoder noted the distinction between war and policing, not in order to endorse it, but in order to illustrate an aspect of a "creeping Empire loyalty" that eventually undermined Christian commitment to pacifism.

As Yoder continued the historical narrative, he moved through the medieval period, in which vestiges of the earlier pacifism lived on in medieval attempts to limit conflicts through the just war theory, to recount how the Reformation welded Christian loyalty to autonomous nation-states and embroiled Europe in ruinous wars of religion. To reduce Reformation violence, a new *secular* internationalism arose that envisioned a world police system to replace warfare.[25] Thus Yoder used policing as a judgment against the mainstream Reformation, which should have restored early Christian pacifism but instead resorted to holy wars.

Finally, Yoder noted that in the early twentieth century, liberal Protestants often called for an international police force to replace warfare as part of their "Puritan vision" to "enforce goodness." Yoder emphasized that these Protestants never examined the implications of this stance. "Other people," he noted, "said that if violence is wrong, an international police force is also wrong."[26] He then critiqued liberal Protestants for not taking sin seriously enough and questioned whether their internationalist vision was "an extreme form of the just war theory."[27] Lacking philosophical and theological depth, they based their pacifism on the presumed reasonableness of their position, and their entire project crumbled with the threat of Hitler. Although liberal Protestants had given details for how an international police force would work,[28] Yoder seems to have deliberately ignored these studies and only used the distinction rhetorically to chide Protestants and Catholics for their Constantinianism.

In fact, in an essay published in 1995, "How Many Ways Are There to Think Morally about War?,"[29] Yoder excoriated those who promised to abolish war and replace it with a world government with policing powers to resolve crises and conflicts. These people "assume that international society is domestic society writ large" and "redefine the notion of 'legitimate authority'" as an international police force.[30] Although James Turner Johnson called this position "utopian pacifism," Yoder protested that "it is inappropriate for Johnson to call this 'pacifism,' since the advocates of this vision regularly justify war . . . in a police role once the world order is established."[31] Yoder claimed a better designation would be "world order visionaries" because "they are not literally 'pacifist' according to any normal meaning of the term."[32]

The striking similarity between current ethical reflection on policing and what Yoder called "world order visionaries" makes it far-fetched that Yoder would be gratified to have his name invoked so frequently within this theory.

Ad Hoc Use of Policing

Thus far I have argued that, for Yoder, the state's police function tempers violence but also creates new opportunities for oppression, and is not a good in which Christians are called to participate. Furthermore, historically when Christians have accepted the distinction between war and policing, it divided their loyalties and led them to dilute New Testament pacifism in internationalist visions or just war theories. He used the distinction mostly as a rhetorical tool with which to rebuke Protestants who grant a blank check to the state and was highly critical of liberal Protestants who advocated an early form of "just policing."

Now I will highlight that Yoder used the distinction in deliberately unsystematic ways. Here are the differences he noted:

- The police do not judge a person's guilt nor do they pronounce a sentence; they only apprehend the perceived offender.[33]
- The police target individual offenders, not entire populations.[34]
- The police arrest individuals for clearly defined crimes.[35]
- The police are accountable to an authority that scrutinizes their violence.[36]
- The police have only enough weaponry to catch the average criminal, instead of an arsenal to wipe out entire populations.[37]

These fragments are gleaned from several sources in which Yoder fleetingly mentions one or more of them. We might question, as I have in other publications,[38] whether these distinctions are as tight as Yoder suggests and note that Yoder did not differentiate between small-town police, city cops, or international police forces. Surely international policing will look a lot more like current wars than small-town local police. At the same time, however, even local police forces are not nearly as benign as Yoder seemed to and just policing advocates do make them out to be. As I argue at length elsewhere, historically and currently the police system has served mostly as a tool for the powerful in racial and class conflict. Thus, even local state police efforts pose serious problems for any attempt to make them a model for reforming the international system.[39]

Yoder's lack of clarity on the differences between international and local policing, however, and his lack of any substantive historical and sociological work on police forces has allowed scholars to use him to develop a more systematic theology than Yoder would have been comfortable with. Yet a close reading of his work reveals that scholars have used his work in this area in a way that distorts his views. Yoder used the criteria I listed above in specific contexts for specific purposes. These *fragments* do not suggest that Yoder employed them to develop a "theology for global police forces" at "the end of his life" as Schlabach and Wallis have suggested. Nor did Yoder emphasize them, as Cortright has claimed.[40] Compiled from varied sources, the list above suggests that he *intentionally* avoided developing a theology or system from the points. In any case, while he periodically referenced policing in the 1970s and early 80s, thereafter the distinction declined dramatically in his works.[41] When Yoder mentioned policing in 1995, he disparaged the idea.

Pacifists and Police Occupations

Although Yoder insisted that Christians should not participate in policing, some have pointed to a passage in *The Christian Witness to the State* to buttress their own arguments that Christians could participate in policing. Yoder asked whether any Christian is called to be an agent of God's wrath in police occupations. He asserted that nonresistance should be the Christian norm and that any person who thought they had a calling to be an agent of God's wrath—that is, a police officer—should "bring to us (i.e., lay before the brotherhood) the evidence that he has such a special calling."[42] Although Yoder claimed he had not met anyone who claimed such a calling, some ethicists now point to this passage and ask whether Yoder would currently affirm that pacifist Christians could become police officers.

Indeed, in *Christian Attitudes to War, Peace and Revolution*, Yoder acknowledged a spectrum of answers to the question, "Can pacifists join an international police force?"

- Some answer no. They view the police as essentially violent and categorically exclude police occupations.
- Some would allow Christians to participate in a completely unarmed police force, or they would participate if they themselves could remain unarmed.
- Those who primarily object to killing would allow Christians to participate if the force were armed with "nonlethal" weapons.
- Those who primarily object to war would join a potentially lethal police force.[43]

At issue is where Yoder placed his own position and where he advocated the most faithful position would be. On this question, scholars have read Yoder in two ways.

Christians could join a potentially lethal police force. Acknowledging that Yoder did not think that Mennonites (i.e., Christian pacifists) should *currently* participate in police forces,[44] Gerald Schlabach interrogates Mennonites who propose that the police become less violent: "*Are you willing to help implement the changes for which you have called? Why then is governance not legitimate for Christians?*"[45] Schlabach evidently believes that Mennonites ought to participate in policing at some future point and never questions whether other Christians should hold those occupations. Yet he does not imagine a "nonviolent" force down the road. He images "some kind of SWAT team with recourse to lethal violence."[46] Based on a private conversation, Schlabach asserts that Yoder might allow Christians to participate in such violence if it were truly an exception.[47] In making this claim, Schlabach implicitly locates Yoder in the fourth option.

In answer to the type of questions Schlabach asks, Yoder stated that Christians should model the prophets. Rather than offering a "detailed plan for the administration of society," Christians should speak "first of all God's condemnation of concrete injustices; if those injustices are corrected, new ones may be tackled."[48] Utopian plans always turn demonic because of their immodest view of human potentiality. Tackling one injustice at a time leads to a permanent prophetic stance in which the word is judgment. Furthermore, Schlabach's assertion that Yoder might allow Christians to participate in a lethal police action seems completely out of Yoder's character. For Yoder discipleship meant "abandonment of all loyalties that counter that obedience [to Christ], including the desire to be effective immediately or to make oneself responsible for civil justice."[49] Those who accuse Christians of complicity in violence for refusing to participate in policing also implicitly accuse God of evil for "letting his innocent Son be killed."[50]

In "Peace Without Eschatology?" Yoder also addressed the accusation that "by not taking over themselves the police function in society Christians would abandon this function to evil people or to the 'demonic.'"[51] Yoder listed four reasons why this accusation is neither biblical nor realistic. First, if Christians leave policing in the hands of others, it does not leave it in the worst possible hands; it leaves the police in Christ's hands. Second, Yoder argued that Christian stories permeate through society with catechesis and other forms of education, so that leavening works better than policing. Third, party politics would subvert the church's prophetic function. Fourth, citing Isaiah 10, in which God used Assyria to check Israel's "egoism" but afterwards judged Assyria for its own pride, Yoder claimed that "the potential corrective power of other egoisms" would "keep any abuse from going too far." Thus Schlabach's use of Yoder seems misleading to say the least.

Christians could participate in nonviolent or nonlethal police actions. Stanley Hauerwas has read Yoder differently. Pointing to Yoder's statement that those who think they have a police calling should let the church examine the claim, Hauerwas argued that for Yoder, "Everything depends upon the character of the society in which one finds oneself as well as the correlative nature of the police."[52] Yoder, according to Hauerwas, did not categorically exclude participation in policing. In a society in which a Christian would not have to carry lethal weapons, a Christian might hear God calling them to policing. Hauerwas interprets Yoder as mainly objecting to police violence. If the police were to become a nonviolent force, Christians might consider it a duty to join.[53] Hauerwas, therefore, thinks Yoder fits in one of the middle positions where Christians could participate in nonlethal police actions.

However, in stating that "every member of the body of Christ" should abandon the desire "to make oneself responsible for civil justice," Yoder did not entertain the idea that Christians should take up the police function, even if they could serve in "nonviolent" positions. In *The Christian Witness to the State*, Yoder argued that there would never be a time when the state is good enough in this fallen world that Christians would run out of complaints.[54] More radically, he even claimed that "a hypothetical just, sober, and modest state would still be in the order of the demonic."[55] He argued that there are a lot of ways Christians can work for the common good that do not involve them in violence, power games, oaths, or other problems that involvement in policing would bring. Moreover, for Yoder, violence is not the sole criterion by which we discern on these issues:

> Behind the difference on the question of violence as well there is a longer series: truth telling and the swearing of oaths, property ownership and accumulation, the use of even nonviolent civil power for selfish purposes. It would thus be improper to describe minority churches as making a hobby of a single issue or two.[56]

Thus Yoder worked with more complex questions about police occupations, which should involve considering how nonviolence itself could be a tool of oppression, the role of oaths, and police protection of property and moneyed interests. The state is not idolatrous because it uses violence, but it uses violence because it is already idolatrous. Nonviolent tactics will not change this. Yoder, therefore, did not simply accept any of the pacifist answers to policing.

Expanding on Yoder: Police, Nonviolence, and Oppression

Yoder claimed that "even nonviolent civil power" can be used "for selfish purposes."[57] He did not develop this idea, but I think it is an important point to keep in mind. Even though just policing is better than unjust policing, as just war is better than unjust war, that does not make it good or right for Christians to join, even if it uses nonviolent techniques. For example, while in the Birmingham city jail, Martin Luther King Jr. lamented the white church's support for the police, but acknowledged that the police had "been rather disciplined in their public handling of the demonstrators. In this sense they have been rather publicly nonviolent."[58] Yet "nonviolence" is not enough to justify a Christian's support of or participation in such a force. King went on to ask why the police had acted nonviolently and answered bluntly, "to preserve the evil system of segregation." Though King consistently argued that means must be commensurate with the end sought, he lamented the use of moral means to preserve an evil end and claimed that "there is no greater treason than to do the right deed for the wrong reason."[59]

In the novel *Brave New World*, Aldous Huxley imagined a system of nonviolent control in which the police would rarely if ever have to use violence to manage populations. The system arose in the twentieth century in reaction to the horrors of war. Six hundred years later, a World State provides a permanent nonviolent solution to the horrors of war: socially and genetically engineered populations. Each person is conditioned physically and psychologically to be happy with their position in life, whether menial workers or managers. The World State promises security in which citizens no longer have to fear violence or suffering at all. The World State delivers that promise. It is a nonviolent technological utopia. At the end of the novel, "the Savage," who did not grow up in the society, becomes so sickened by the conformity that he tries to help set them free by throwing out a supply of drugs that help keep people conditioned. When a riot breaks out, police armed with sedative filled "water pistols" nonviolently break up the riot while "the Voice of Reason" proclaims over a loudspeaker, "At peace, at peace."[60] Seconds later, the rioters embrace in friendship. The police arrest the Savage responsible for the riot, threatening him only with sedation if he did not comply. In Huxley's novel, the police no longer need to kill or to physically harm a person at all. Yet they uphold a system that is fundamentally evil.[61]

These examples, one real and the other imaginative, illustrate that nonviolence cannot be the sole criterion for determining whether or not we can or will participate in the nation-state's projects.[62] As Romand Coles responded to Hauerwas:

> Lots of what I fear most in "-ocracies" of our day is "nonviolent." Shopping malls . . . are nonviolent, I suppose, but are hell-bent on absorbing every corpuscular of flesh-desire that enters them, to largely—though not simply—odious ends. They seek to rule. Exclude the violence of sweatshops and they'd still be odious.[63]

Nonviolence is not the sole criterion, not merely because nonviolence can be a tool for oppression but because there are other fundamental issues at stake: ecclesiological concerns, oaths, truth-telling, idolatry, and other issues must also be carefully and seriously considered.[64] Yoder's thought, I believe, pointed in this direction as well.

Conclusion

Yoder's legacy challenges us to move toward faithfulness to Christ. Although he distinguished between policing and war, he did not develop a theory or theology out of the distinction. Nor by this distinction did he mean to justify Christian participation in policing. Most scholars who have cited Yoder on this topic have not been careful in their citations and have not taken into account the wider context of his thought. They have therefore tended to exaggerate his intentions in making the distinction between war and policing and have legitimated the state and policing as a Christian calling in a way that Yoder did not.

I have attempted to show that Yoder used "policing" as a conceptual tool—Yoder would have said a "utopian" idea—to critique the present.[65] Such an account, however, need not develop into a theory about how to move from the present to some non-existent place. So Yoder was intentionally unsystematic in his discussion about policing. Furthermore, Yoder attempted to answer outside of the standard pacifist responses to the question of whether Christians should participate in policing. His response, unlike the standard responses, took into account a more robust set of concerns than simply asking how nonviolent the police are. With this wider set of concerns in mind, we would do well to reexamine the nostrum of just policing. In any case, the fundamental question for those who tell us policing is nonviolent is "But do we see Jesus?"

Notes

1. Jim Wallis, "Hard Questions for Peacemakers," *Sojourners*, January/February 2002, 32. See also Jim Wallis, *God's Politics: Why the Right Gets It Wrong and the Left Doesn't Get It* (San Francisco: HarperSanFrancisco, 2005), 164-65. Also in an online interview with Stanley Hauerwas, Wallis asked, "What was John Howard Yoder doing with the ethics of a global police force near the end of his life?" Stanley Hauerwas said he did not know. See Jim Wallis, "Interview with Stanley Hauerwas," *Sojonet: Faith, Politics and Culture*, November 8, 2001, http://www.sojo.net/index.cfm?action=news.display_archives&mode= current_opinion&article=CO_010702h. Accessed June 25, 2008.

2. See Gerald Schlabach, "Just Policing: How War Could Cease to be a Church-Dividing Issue," in *Just Policing: Mennonite-Catholic Theological Colloquium, 2002*, ed. Ivan J. Kauffman (Kitchener, ON: Pandora Press, 2004).

3. Ibid., 60 n9.

4. Glen Stassen and David Gushee, *Kingdom Ethics: Following Jesus in Contemporary Context* (Downers Grove, IL: InterVarsity Press, 2003), 166-67. Tobias Winright has examined Yoder's writings most thoroughly to date. Yet his essay was not systematic and therefore his conclusion about Yoder's stance might be slightly off. See Tobias Winright, "From Police Officers to Peace Officers," in *The Wisdom of the Cross: Essays in Honor of John Howard Yoder*, ed. Stanley Hauerwas, et al (Grand Rapids, MI: Eerdmans, 1999), 108-14. Other references where scholars mention Yoder in relationship to the war/police distinction include: Rose Marie Berger, "A Responsibility to Protect," *Sojourners*, December 2006, 9; Lisa Sowle Cahill, "Just War Theory, Pacifism, and Politics," *Journal of Religious Ethics* 33, no. 4 (2005): 821; William T. Cavanaugh, "Terrorist Enemies and Just War Theory," *Christian Reflection: A Series in Faith and Ethics*, July 2004, 31; David Cortright, *Gandhi and Beyond: Nonviolence for an Age of Terrorism* (Boulder, CO: Paradigm Publishers, 2006), 212; Mark Christopher Kiley, *Colossians as Pseudepigraphy* (Sheffield, UK: JSOT Press, 1986), 133; Edward LeRoy Long, *Facing Terrorism: Responding as Christians* (Louisville, KY: Westminster John Knox Press, 2004), 82-84; William Werpehowski, *American Protestant Ethics and the Legacy of H. Richard Niebuhr* (Washington, D.C.: Georgetown University Press, 2002), 98; Tobias Winright, "Just Cause and Preemptive Strikes in the War on Terrorism: Insights from a Just-Policing Perspective," *Journal of the*

Society of Christian Ethics 26, no. 2 (2006): 164; J. Philip Wogaman, *Christian Perspectives on Politics*, rev. and expanded ed. (Louisville, KY: Westminster John Knox Press, 2000), 69-70; finally see numerous references to Yoder in *At Peace and Unafraid: Public Order, Security, and the Wisdom of the Cross*, ed. Duane K. Friesen and Gerald Schlabach (Scottdale, PA: Herald Press, 2005).

5. David Cortright, *Peace: A History of Movements* (New York: Cambridge University Press, 2008), 14 (emphasis added). See also 177.

6. Ibid., 15. "Peace operations," as we shall see, is not how Yoder would have described these activities.

7. Ibid., 16.

8. In this paper, I do not equate oppression with violence. Oppression, as I am using it, involves economic, social, and psychological exploitation of others that results in one group living off of the resources of another group whose living conditions are significantly lower than the oppressive group. This can be nonviolent in its strategy. The police, I contend, are part of an oppressive state system that maintains and exploits racial, class, and gender inequalities.

9. John Howard Yoder, *The Christian Witness to the State* (Newton, KS: Faith and Life Press, 1964). This book was a revised form of an earlier essay that Yoder wrote in 1955 entitled, "The Theological Basis of the Christian Witness to the State," (Mennonite Historical Library, 1955). Most of what he said about policing was already present in this 1955 paper which he wrote in Basel, Switzerland.

10. Yoder, *The Christian Witness to the State*, 36-37.

11. Ibid., 48. Yoder identifies the crusade concept with Franklin Roosevelt's position in World War II.

12. Ibid., 37.

13. Ibid., 46.

14. Ibid., 48.

15. Ibid., 59.

16. See for example Jeff Gingrich, "Breaking the Uneasy Silence: Policing and the Peace Movement in Dialogue," in *At Peace and Unafraid: Public Order, Security, and the Wisdom of the Cross*, ed. Duane K. Friesen and Gerald Schlabach (Scottdale, PA: Herald Press, 2005), 396; and Maurice Martin, "Police Officers Focus on Peace Role," *Canadian Mennonite*, December 22, 2003.

17. John Howard Yoder, *The Politics of Jesus*, 2nd ed. (Grand Rapids, MI: Eerdmans, 1994), 194.

18. Ibid., 198.

19. Ibid., 203. Yoder anachronistically uses a category of "police" for Greco-Roman antiquity, which had no police whatsoever. Police are a modern invention unknown for most of history.

20. Ibid., 204.

21. Ibid., 202-3. By "nonresistant" Yoder did not mean acquiescence to evil nor did he mean to exclude all opposition to evil. See 202 n14.

22. John Howard Yoder, *Christian Attitudes to War, Peace and Revolution*, ed. Ted Koontz and Andy Alexis-Baker (Grand Rapids, MI: Brazos Press, 2009), 50.

23. Ibid. Yoder also claims that these soldiers were probably "excused from the oath and the ceremonies" (31). In his early church narrative, Yoder followed Bainton: see Roland H. Bainton, *Christian Attitudes Toward War and Peace* (New York: Abingdon Press, 1960), 79-81. However Bainton did not claim that soldiers were dispensed from the oath. Bainton cited Baillie Reynolds, *The Vigiles of Imperial Rome* (London: Oxford University Press, 1926). The vigiles were a military fire-brigade in Rome and Reynolds claims that "whether the force as originally constituted took a military oath or not is uncertain" (65). If Yoder checked some of Bainton's references in the footnotes and read this book, then he presented a slightly more optimistic portrait in saying that the force was "probably" dispensed from the oath rather than Reynolds' cautionary "it is uncertain." In fact most scholars who have researched the *cohortes praetoriae*, the *vigiles*, or the *cohortes urbanae*, which were all military units who functioned other than as warriors in battle, do not paint such a peaceful picture of these units' activities. For other sources available to Yoder at the time that make a different argument than Yoder and Bainton see Marcel Durry, *Les cohortes prétoriennes* (Paris: E. de Boccard, 1938); Edward Echols, "The Roman City Police: Origin and Development," *The Classical Journal* 53, no. 8 (1958); and Ramsay MacMullen, *Enemies of the Roman Order: Treason, Unrest, and Alienation in the Empire* (Cambridge, MA: Harvard University Press, 1966), 163-91.

24. John Howard Yoder, *The Priestly Kingdom* (Notre Dame, IN: University of Notre Dame Press, 1984), 74-75.

25. Yoder, *Christian Attitudes to War, Peace and Revolution*, 214-15.

26. Ibid., 283.

27. Ibid.

28. For example see the systematic treatment of the subject in David Davies, *The Problem of the Twentieth Century: A Study in International Relationships* (New York: Putnam, 1931), 360-501; Charles Reith, *Police Principles and the Problem of War* (London: Oxford University Press, 1940).

29. John Howard Yoder, "How Many Ways Are There to Think Morally about War?" *Journal of Law and Religion* 11, no. 1 (1994): 83-107.

30. Ibid., 101.

31. Ibid., 98-99.

32. Ibid., 100, 101.

33. Yoder, *The Christian Witness to the State*, 47; and *Discipleship as Political Responsibility* (Scottdale, PA: Herald Press, 2003), 77.

34. Yoder, *Christian Attitudes to War, Peace and Revolution*, 282; *The Christian Witness to the State*, 47; *Discipleship as Political Responsibility*, 77; and *The Politics of Jesus*, 204.

35. Yoder, *The Christian Witness to the State*, 47.

36. Yoder, *Christian Attitudes to War, Peace and Revolution*, 80-81; and *The Politics of Jesus*, 204.

37. Yoder, *The Politics of Jesus*, 204. In addition, Yoder mentions policing without enumerating any differences between it and war in John Howard Yoder, *Nevertheless: A Meditation on the Varieties and Shortcomings of Religious Pacifism*, revised and expanded ed. (Scottdale, PA: Herald Press, 1992), 44, 45.

38. I do not intend to critique these distinctions in this paper. For my sustained critiques of just policing and suggestions on the way congregations can begin to lessen their dependence upon the police, see Andy Alexis-Baker, "The Gospel or a Glock?: Mennonites and the Police," *Conrad Grebel Review* 25, no. 2 (2007): 23-49; "Community, Policing and Violence," *Conrad Grebel Review* 26, no. 2 (2008): 102-16; and "Just Policing: A New Face to an Old Challenge," in *Church at Peace in a World at War*, ed. Michael Hardin (Telford, PA: Cascadia, forthcoming).

39. It does not solve the problem, as Gerald Schlabach recently suggested, to divorce "policing" from the "police" because just policing advocates are not claiming that a teacher "policing" a classroom is a model for warfare. That is absurd to argue, stretching the term beyond usability and dialogue. See Gerald Schlabach, "Just the Police Function, Then: Reply to Alexis-Baker," *Conrad Grebel Review* 26, no. 2 (2008).

In any case, when Yoder used the concepts of "policing" or the "police function" of the state, he clearly had in mind police forces as an institution and structure.

40. David Cortright, *Gandhi and Beyond*, 212.

41. Furthermore, although *Christian Attitudes to War, Peace and Revolution* and *When War Is Unjust* narrate a historical overview of Christians and war, Yoder does not mention "police action" as analogous to the justifiable war tradition in the latter work. If he had been developing a theory out of policing at the end of his life, as Jim Wallis and Gerald Schlabach have alleged, the 1996 revision of *When War is Unjust* should have at least mentioned the distinction. Although Yoder did not make the distinction, the author of the foreword did. See Charles P. Lutz, "Foreword to the First Edition," in *When War Is Unjust*, xiii.

42. Yoder, *The Christian Witness to the State*, 56-57. These comments were not in the 1955 essay, "The Theological Basis of the Christian Witness to the State."

43. Yoder, *Christian Attitudes to War, Peace, and Revolution*, 215. Tobias Winright follows a slightly different typology than Yoder. See Winright, "From Police Officers to Peace Officers," 96-108.

44. Schlabach, "Just Policing," 39. "If Yoder was moving the discussion of policing from the domain of principle to the domain of vocational discernment, the immediate result was not to make it any more likely that Christian pacifists would apply to become police officers. Rather, Yoder drove home the point that the *conditions do not now exist to make this morally possible*" (emphasis added).

45. Ibid., 47, 48. See also Wogaman, *Christian Perspectives on Politics*, 69.

46. Schlabach, "Just Policing," 59.

47. Schlabach claims that in a private conversation Yoder "allowed that he would be ready to consider limited exceptions against violence if he became convinced . . . that such exceptions really were exceptions." Ibid., 124. I question whether Schlabach was wise to publish this comment given that Yoder was not alive to clarify Schlabach's assertions. Nevertheless, as stated Schlabach's sentence is ambiguous. The word "violence" here does not mean "killing," and he left it ambiguous whether Yoder allowed that *Christians* could participate in exceptional and limited "violence" (but not killing). Everything Yoder published suggests that his answer was an unqualified "no" to Christians and killing.

So Schlabach's SWAT scenario would exclude Christians in Yoder's understanding.

48. Yoder, "Peace Without Eschatology," in *The Royal Priesthood*, ed. Michael Cartwright (Grand Rapids, MI: Eerdmans, 1994), 161. This essay was published three other times: John Howard Yoder, "If Christ Is Truly Lord," in *The Original Revolution* (Scottdale, PA: Herald Press, 1971); *Peace Without Eschatology*, Concern (Akron, OH: Concern, 1961). All citations will be from the 1994 edition since it is most accessible.

49. Ibid., 158.

50. Ibid., 151.

51. Ibid., 163. All other quotes that I use from this essay are from the same page.

52. Stanley Hauerwas, "Can A Pacifist Think About War?" in *Dispatches from the Front* (Durham, NC: Duke University Press, 1994), 128.

53. Ibid., 128-29. See also Hauerwas's comments in his book *A Better Hope* (Grand Rapids, MI: Brazos Press, 2000), 280 n19.

54. Yoder, *The Christian Witness to the State*, 32.

55. Ibid., 37 n.8.

56. John Howard Yoder, "Radical Reformation Ethics in Ecumenical Perspective," in *The Priestly Kingdom*, 111.

57. Yoder, *The Christian Witness to the State*, 32.

58. Martin Luther King, "Letter from Birmingham City Jail," in *A Testament of Hope: The Essential Writings and Speeches of Martin Luther King Jr.*, ed. James Melvin Washington (San Francisco: HarperSanFrancisco, 1991), 301.

59. Ibid.

60. See Aldous Huxley, *Brave New World* (London: Chatto & Windus, 1964), chapter 15.

61. For other novels that imagine nonviolent technological societies that resemble Huxley's dystopia see Lois Lowry, *The Giver* (New York: Bantam Books, 1999) and Robert Theobald, *Teg's 1994* (Chicago: Swallow Press, 1972). The point here is that *nonviolent tactics* in the hands of an oppressive system are nonviolent oppressive tactics. Nonviolence changes little of the technological system.

62. I want to make clear that I am not saying that nonviolence is unimportant, only that focusing *solely* on this question distorts the nature of Christian reasoning.

63. Stanley Hauerwas and Romand Coles, *Christianity, Democracy, and the Radical Ordinary* (Eugene, OR: Cascade Books, 2008), 39.

64. Yoder makes idolatry an issue in Yoder, *The Christian Witness to the State*, 15. For oaths, see Yoder, *Christian Attitudes to War, Peace and Revolution*, 44-45, 180-83. For how the Bible might call into question the police bureaucracy, see Yoder, *Discipleship as Political Responsibility*, 36-37.

65. Yoder, "How Many Ways Are There to Think Morally about War?" 99.

Chapter 10

Biblical Warfare Revisited:
Extending the Insights of John Howard Yoder

John C. Nugent

The past few decades have seen the proliferation of essays and full-length monographs addressing the problem of warfare in Scripture.[1] Though these works approach the subject in multiple ways, they present only three basic options.[2] *Duality* approaches accentuate the discontinuity between the testaments and call Christians to follow the New, not the Old.[3] *Plurality* approaches argue that the Old Testament conveys a debate between competing views and note that Jesus settles the debate in favor of nonviolence.[4] *Continuity* approaches assert that God was working even in the Old Testament to limit bloodshed and that the New Testament work of Christ marks the decisive break.[5] In all their diversity, the above three options narrate the problem of biblical warfare[6] in such a way that the critical turning point takes place with the proclamation of Jesus, thereby driving a wedge between the testaments.

At precisely this point John Howard Yoder enters the conversation with critical insights that, to my knowledge, have not been sufficiently engaged. In particular, Yoder narrated Israel's history in such a way that, long before Jesus, God reconfigured Israel's life and mission so that warfare would become obsolete. In this essay I argue that this narration, with significant alterations, helps answer the challenge warfare poses for biblical ethics.

Yoder's Evolving Understanding of Israelite History and Warfare

Yoder's first two works on Israelite warfare emphasize continuity. In "If Abraham is Our Father," Yoder critiques four approaches to biblical warfare before presenting his own which analyzes the "concrete historical anthropological meaning" of challenging passages. He claims that such passages—like the Akedah or near-slaying of Isaac—do not teach that killing is moral in certain kinds of situations but that God's people must rely on his provision for their safety in all situations.[7] Following Millard Lind and others,[8] Yoder argues that the holy war into which God enlisted Israel taught the Israelites to trust neither military might nor human strategy but to follow God's instructions and wait upon his deliverance. In *The Politics of Jesus*, Yoder restates the above case and buttresses the continuity position by noting that when Israel took warfare into its own hands the results were often disastrous.[9] This dismal track record serves as a biblical commentary on what happens when Israel abandons the holy war posture.

In the last two decades of his life, however, Yoder began focusing on the significance of Jewish history for understanding the nature and origin of Christian nonviolence.[10] This work yielded a revised understanding of the Babylonian exile that produced ripple effects in all directions.[11] If Yoder's interpretation of the exile is correct, then both the pre-exilic and post-exilic periods should be understood in ways that reframe the issue of biblical warfare. As far as I can tell, Yoder's clarion call for such a revision is first sounded (in print) in Yoder's brief introduction to Millard Lind's *Yahweh is a Warrior*.[12] Yoder begins by laying out the "near-marcionite" manner by which some scholars discuss biblical warfare and then remarks: "The total interpretive *Gestalt* just sketched needs revision from every angle: the underlying anti-Judaism, the imperial establishment mood, the failure to perceive in the Hebrew scriptures the evolution from Joshua to Jeremiah, and in postcolonial Judaism the further evolution through Jochanan ben Zakkai to Judah 'the Prince.'"[13] From this point forward, this evolution from Joshua to Jeremiah becomes central to Yoder's project.

In "Jesus the Jewish Pacifist," a lecture delivered two years later, Yoder explains his conviction that since Jeremiah, the Israelites took on a form of existence that lent itself to pacifism and was consistent with Israel's prior conviction that God would fight for them. When Jeremiah advised the Israelites to accept the yoke of Babylon and make themselves at home in exile (Jer 29:4-7), he was not simply sharing practical skills for surviving a temporary whirlwind of divine judgment; he was permanently reconfiguring and repositioning Israel for transterritorial existence and global mission. The exiled Jews ceased to be a people of the city (Jerusalem) and of the soil (Palestine) and became a people of the book (Torah). They needed neither a centralized cult with its sacrificial system and priestly supports nor a centralized government with its royal court and military backing. They found creative ways to maintain their identity as God's people on foreign soil. This exiled status did not end with the Persia-sponsored return, restructure, and refortification. The Jews did not return to claim their own land and realize God's promises; they returned to occupy a Persian province in ways approved by the Persian overlord. This Jeremianic turn not only laid the groundwork for Israel's new social shape, but it clinched Yoder's case for a negative estimation of Israel's monarchical project with its standing army:

> Already in the histories of the age of Gideon and Jotham, Samuel and Saul, the recognition of JHWH as a warrior and king had led to rejecting not accepting the notion that Israel should adopt the institution of kingship "like the other nations." The later review of that national story by the prophets became still more critical of kingship. National independence was forfeited, first in the North and then in Judaea as well, because of the unwillingness of the kings and the people to trust God for their national survival. With Jeremiah God abandoned kingship as a vehicle of his people's identity. With Ezra and Nehemiah the return to live and worship in Judaea was brought about without political independence or a king. The Maccabean adventure, although militarily successful for a time, ultimately further discredited the holy war vision. The texts of Esther and Daniel . . . fill out the picture of the faithful life that can be lived under pagan kings.[14]

This basic schema is either presumed or further spelled out in all of Yoder's subsequent works on this subject. In 1989 he published his last full-length article on holy war in which, after restating his conviction that God does the fighting in such wars, he goes on to say that the people's responsibility to trust in JHWH alone took on a sociological form in which David—not Diaspora—was the detour.[15] In 1992 Yoder wrote a brief response to Michael Walzer's de-historicizing approach that reduces the holy wars of Israel to a later Deuteronomic rewrite.[16] Yoder faults Walzer for ignoring the cultic dimensions of holy war and for positing a revision of history that is unconvincing and raises more problems than it solves. His most relevant objection to Walzer's approach, however, is that it fails to account for the fact that the Jeremianic vision, which chronologically spans the exile and beyond, has more in common with the earlier holy war tradition than it does the monarchical project that de-historicists make central. Having ignored Jeremiah, de-historicists embrace the exception—monarchy with its standing army—and make it the rule.

Through such sundry essays we could begin to piece together Yoder's answer to the problem of biblical warfare, yet Yoder spells it out most fully in his final lecture on this topic, delivered in 1995: "See How They Go with Their Face to the Sun." In this essay Yoder makes explicit that Jeremiah is the turning point of Jewish history, not only in the biblical narrative but beyond:

> More than Christians are aware, Babylon itself very soon became the cultural center of world Jewry, from the age of Jeremiah until the time we in the West call the Middle Ages. The people who re-colonized the "Land of Israel," repeatedly, from the age of Jeremiah to that of Jochanan ben Zakkai, and again still later, were supported financially and educationally from Babylon, and in lesser ways from the rest of the diaspora. Our palestinocentric reading of the story is a mistake, though a very understandable one. . . . In all the different ways represented by Sadducees, Pharisees, Maccabeans and Essenes, Jews in Palestine had no choice but to define their identity over against the dominant Gentiles and to be divided from one another by their conflicting responses to that challenge. On the other hand, the synagogues and rabbis in Babylon, and in the rest of the world where the Babylonian model was followed and the Babylonian teachers were consulted, were spared that self-defeating distraction, so as to enter into creatively that Jeremianic phase of creating something qualitatively new in the history of religions.[17]

That "something qualitatively new" was a faith community with at least four defining attributes. First, they took directives not from centralized headquarters but from a copyable text that could be read anywhere. Second, a local cell need comprise only ten households without priesthood and hierarchy. Third, they sustained international unity through intervisitation, intermarriage, commerce, and rabbinic consultation. Fourth, their common life or walk as shaped by their story served as the ground floor of their identity.[18]

These attributes are remarkably similar to post-Pentecost churches, which is precisely Yoder's point. The duality, plurality, and standard continuity approaches rightly affirm that Jesus signaled an era in world history during which God's people did not need the sword to secure and sustain their identity, but God's people could and should have left the sword behind long before. If Yoder is right that the monarchical phase was not the center of Jewish history but an unfortunate detour, then warfare is not truly an Old versus New Testament issue but one contained within the Old Testament itself.

Having identified the nature of the Jeremianic shift as Yoder construes it, it is necessary to step back and survey how this shift fits within the overall biblical story. Yoder never narrates the entire story at once, but for the sake of clarity I have pulled together various strands and filled in a few gaps to present a coherent reading worth engaging.

1. Bloodshed immediately followed the Fall (Gen 4:1-16), precipitated the flood (Gen 6:1-8), and was outlawed immediately thereafter (Gen 9:5-6).
2. God called Abraham to form a people whose identity pivoted around the principle that God alone can create and sustain his people, so taking matters into their own hands is a grave mistake.[19]
3. Israel's deliverance from Egypt was entirely God's work (Exod 14:25, 31) and the holy wars by which God gave Israel the land reinforced the centrality of God's work to the exclusion of normal human means and motivations for warfare.
4. Whenever Israel entered warfare *as the nations around them did* the results were often disastrous, so the holy war posture of national security remained normative until the monarchy.
5. Though the kingship was decried by Gideon and Jotham (Judg 8:22–9:25), and Samuel and God (1 Sam 8:6-8), God reluctantly granted Israel's request for a king and warned them of its negative consequences (1 Sam 8:9-22).[20]
6. Israel's kings were at their best when they relied on God's deliverance (e.g., Ahaz and Hezekiah) and at their worst when they played the military game (e.g., David and Josiah). But overall the kingship lived

up to its negative expectations and the prophets disparaged it (Hos 13:11).[21]

7. Through Jeremiah, God called Israel out of its self-imposed monarchical cul-de-sac and into a dynamic new scattered posture that was conducive to blessing the nations.

8. The exilic guidelines Jeremiah set forth were appropriate not only for life in Babylon but also back in Palestine, so all efforts to reestablish monarchial existence in Palestine after Cyrus' decree were doomed to fail.[22]

9. Finally, facing the severe second-century persecutions of Antiochus Epiphanes, the book of Daniel largely ignores the Maccabeans' violent revolt and encourages the Jews to remain radically faithful to the point of death and to wait patiently for divine deliverance (Dan 7:11-14).[23]

It will not do, therefore, to say that Old Testament Israel needed the sword because it was a nation-state and that the New Testament church does not because it isn't. Rather, the message of the Old Testament is that Israel should never have adopted a position that required the sword—most concretely manifested in a standing army as opposed to ad hoc forces gathered for divinely specified purposes. Moreover, for most of its history, the Israelites were not an independent nation, backed by a royal army, but sojourners or subjects under foreign rule who were forced to rely on God alone.[24]

Yoder's account raises some important questions. Why would God allow something like the monarchy? Why would he stick by his people and work with them despite their choosing a style of leadership and mode of being in the world that was doomed to fail? Why would God fight military battles for his people at all if he did not want them to become a people accustomed to military battles? These are important questions that rise to the surface once Israel's history is revised as Yoder suggests. But is his revision tenable?

Engaging and Revising Yoder's Narration of Biblical History

Yoder's revision of biblical history has received little scholarly attention and what it has received has been mostly critical, even by those sympathetic with Yoder's overall project. In a tribute to Yoder's life, A. James Reimer notes that Yoder's account is driven by his free-church agenda and fails to do justice to the importance of organized, institutional, religious, and political life in Judaism.[25] Peter Ochs, a Jewish scholar, accuses Yoder of building a "beautiful monument of one chapter of Jeremiah's ministry" that cannot be supported by the remaining chapters of Jeremiah.[26] He further faults Yoder for setting up a problematic dichotomy between landedness and exiled existence that fails to capture the essence of Jewish thought, which holds the two together.

John Goldingay, in his 2003 *Old Testament Theology*, pejoratively remarks in passing that "Yoder's anti-Ezra-ism is the left hand of his Christology."[27] More sympathetic is an Evangelical Theological Society paper by Old Testament scholar Paul J. Kissling that affirms Yoder's attempt to glean fruit from Israel's diasporic identity while seeking to retain the importance of post-exilic Palestinian existence in ways that are compatible with Yoder's overall theological project.[28] Kissling faults Yoder's account for interpreting Ezra poorly, reading second-temple Judaism selectively, ignoring the already-but-not-yet nature of the sixth-century return to Palestine, imposing a needless dichotomy between Palestinian centralization and diasporic existence, and overreacting to sacerdotalism.

This somewhat cold scholarly reception raises three fundamental questions that Yoder's narration must answer if it is to gain a fair hearing and provide helpful insight for answering questions about biblical warfare. (1) Can Yoder's reading of Jeremiah be maintained? (2) Do post-exilic biblical texts truly support Yoder's thesis? (3) Does Yoder do justice to the manifold nature of post-exilic Judaism?

From a purely historicist perspective, the answer to all three questions is probably no. Jeremiah likely expected Israel to return to the land in style and to reestablish Jerusalem in such a way that all nations would stream to it for instruction.[29] He probably viewed the exile as yet another detour along the way to Israel's palestinocentric future glory. Likewise, the authors of Ezra, Nehemiah, and the post-exilic prophets probably imagined that God would soon fully restore Jerusalem far beyond the anti-climactic restoration they had witnessed.[30] Furthermore, a careful reading of second temple Jewish literature yields a rich variety of perspectives within Judaism, some of which affirm the sixth-century restoration project and others that ignore or disparage it.[31]

But all of this misses Yoder's point. Yoder is neither a professed Jew who reads Israel's history primarily in light of subsequent rabbinic development nor an Old Testament scholar who locates the text's meaning primarily in authorial intent. He is a Christocentric, postliberal, biblical realist who reads all of Scripture and history in light of God's definitive revelation of his ultimate purposes in Christ and his church.[32] For Yoder, then, the fact that the Messiah had already come and distanced himself from the Jerusalem establishment, the fact that the Messiah did not reconstitute Israel as a palestinocentric community of faith but prepared them to be scattered throughout the world by his Spirit, and the fact that previously scattered Jews as far back as Jeremiah formed synagogues throughout the world that became central to the church's missionary expansion cannot be ignored. In short, the strength in Yoder's position lies not in sixth-century prophecy and history but in the first-century revelation of God's purposes through the Messiah, Holy Spirit, and church. From Yoder's perspective, we ought to ask not only what Jeremiah and Ezra thought they were saying to sixth-century Jews but also what God is saying through them to post-Pentecost Christians.

This defense notwithstanding, Yoder's critics have exposed at least one major weakness that manifests itself in multiple ways, namely, Yoder's needlessly pejorative reading of palestinocentric existence, the city of Jerusalem, and the return from exile.[33] This weakness needs to be addressed for three biblical reasons. First and foremost is God's promise to Abraham in Genesis 12:1-3. Central to this promise is God's commitment to lead Abraham and his descendents into the Promised Land. This is no mere subtheme. The entire literary plot of Torah—the core of the Jewish canon—revolves around God's commitment to settling Abraham and his descendents in Canaan, where he will bless them and position them to be a blessing to the nations.[34] Yoder never engages this critical aspect of the Old Testament story.

Second, late Old Testament and early Christian texts consistently accord Jerusalem a place of special honor. Ezekiel's glorious vision of a restored Jerusalem and temple is the most elaborate palestinocentric vision of hope in the Old Testament (Ezek 40–48). Zechariah also envisions Israel's future hope in terms of Jerusalem's exaltation (Zech 2:1-5; 8:1-8; 14:3-21). Even Daniel's act of civil disobedience preserves what may have been a common Jewish practice of praying toward Jerusalem (Dan 6:10). These are important witnesses since Ezekiel, Zechariah, and Daniel stand out among late Old Testament texts in corroborating Yoder's thesis that post-exilic Israel recovered the practice of not taking matters into their own hands but relying solely on JHWH's deliverance.[35]

That reverence for Jerusalem continued into the common era is evident on a small scale in Mary and Joseph's annual pilgrimage to Jerusalem to celebrate the Passover (Luke 2:41) and on a large scale when thousands of Jews responded to the gospel message because they had flocked to Jerusalem to celebrate Pentecost (Acts 2). This practice may not have stopped for Jewish Christians as evident in the apostle Paul's desire late in life to visit Jerusalem to celebrate Pentecost (Acts 20:16).[36] Jesus also acknowledged Jerusalem's importance, although not until the end of his life—and this with good reason. After his resurrection, Jesus told his disciples:

> "These are my words that I spoke to you while I was still with you—that everything written about me in the law of Moses, the prophets, and the psalms must be fulfilled." Then he opened their minds to understand the scriptures, and he said to them, "Thus it is written, that the Messiah is to suffer and to rise from the dead on the third day, and that repentance and forgiveness of sins is to be proclaimed in his name to all nations, *beginning from Jerusalem.* (Luke 24:44-47, NRSV)[37]

Earthly Jerusalem thus played an important role not only in Jewish eschatology but also in Jesus' death and the church's mission.[38]

Third, though post-exilic biblical texts portray the return from exile somewhat negatively as falling short of Israel's grand expectations (Ezra 3:10-13; Neh 9:36; and Hag 2:1-3), they nonetheless also narrate it positively as the providential act of God. Ezra and Nehemiah both see God's hand working mightily in their initial return, refortification, and reform projects (Ezra 7:6, 9, 28; 8:23; Neh 2:12, 18, 20; 4:15; 6:16; 12:43). Likewise, the prophets Haggai and Zechariah discern God's direct involvement in the temple rebuilding under the "messianic" leadership of Zerubbabel and Joshua (Hag 1:7-14; Zech 3:1–4:14; 6:9-15; 8:1-14). Though many Jews of this time may have over-estimated the eschatological significance of these events, there is little reason to deny Scripture's testimony that God was instrumental in reestablishing the post-exilic community.

In light of the foundational significance of the Promised Land, the ongoing relevance of Jerusalem, and the providential oversight of the return from exile, I submit a fourfold revision of Yoder's narration. First, rather than ignore the Abrahamic promise, I recommend we regard it as a constitutive phase in God's plan for Israel. This plan began with one man and his wife and ultimately culminated in a numerous people with a distinct identity scattered throughout the world bearing witness to God's kingdom. But how could God move Israel from its humble origins to this grand fulfillment? A first necessary step was to multiply Abraham's offspring in such a way that they would not lose their identity. Egypt was an ideal incubator. God's people multiplied there, albeit under adverse conditions, with little interference from the Egyptians since they refused to intermingle with lowly Semite shepherds (Gen 46:33-34).

However, not just any kind of distinct identity would suffice. Israel's identity must reflect God's ultimate will for creation. This could not happen in bondage, so God temporarily relocated the Israelites to Palestine, where they could order their lives according to Torah, which reflected God's will for all creation in a contextually appropriate manner. As far as the Israelites knew, this was the last phase. Once they rightly ordered their lives and received God's blessing, they expected the nations to stream to them and that God's purposes would be fulfilled. But this did not happen.[39] One way to explain its lack of fulfillment is to say that Israel failed so God switched plans and moved in a transterritorial direction beginning with the Diaspora and continuing with the church in Acts. Another way is to say that, despite the Israelites' failings, God worked through their bad choices (including a monarchy like the nations) to bring about his prior intention of scattering them in preparation for the equipping and sending of the messianic community. Interpreted in this way, temporary centralized existence in Palestine need not threaten the critical role diaspora would later play in the life of Israel and the church.

Second, rather than regard the Jeremianic turn as the definitive break from palestinocentric faith, I recommend we regard it as the *initial embrace* of diaspora as a way of life. This new way would not end with the sixth-century return from exile nor the first-century advent of the Messiah. Indeed, diaspora paved the way for the church's own exiled existence.[40] This beginning of the new need not entail the decisive ending of the old, although the nature of Jerusalem's on-going significance does change.

Third, rather than regard the return from exile as a failed restoration, I recommend we view it as the successful reestablishment of Jerusalem as one city among many where Jews must forge a new communal existence under pagan imperial oversight. It may have been the end of exile for some,[41] but it nonetheless meant cultivating a social identity in Palestine that had more in common with diasporic existence than the glorious restoration envisioned by the prophets. The anticlimactic return is pivotal and providential because had the Jews not been permitted to return, it would have been tempting for them to hold out hope that all would be well if only they could somehow return to Palestine. The anti-climactic return thus legitimized diasporic existence by debunking hopes of fully reclaiming Jerusalem without the kind of dramatic divine intervention envisioned in Daniel.[42]

Fourth, in light of the ongoing respect paid to Jerusalem in both testaments, I recommend narrating Jerusalem's ongoing significance in terms of an "eschatological home base." This perspective mirrors that of Revelation and stands in fundamental continuity with the Old Testament prophets. Jews and Christians who embrace diasporic existence need not forget about Jerusalem. It remains a powerful symbol that helps God's people imagine what glory God has in store. If David could build a glorious city within Israel, how much more glorious will be the city whose architect and builder is God (Heb 11:10).

Conclusion

This revised Yoderian narration of the biblical story both strengthens Yoder's position against justified criticism and uniquely positions us to meet the challenge of biblical warfare. It remains now to apply this narration specifically to warfare, which I do in five stages:

1. From the very beginning Israel's God was against bloodshed.[43]
2. When God's plan required temporarily constituting Israel as a territorial people, God pioneered a form of warfare that placed initiative and responsibility for bloodshed on his own shoulders and required the Israelites to trust primarily in his miraculous provision.
3. God warned his people to avoid the war-making ways of monarchy, and when they ignored this warning he allowed their ill-fated experiment to collapse under the weight of its own inadequacies.
4. As the kingship crumbled, God began repositioning his people for their new phase in his mission. Through exile he began scattering them throughout the world. Through prophets like Jeremiah and leaders like Ezra and Nehemiah, he helped them acclimate themselves to their new status as a non-militant minority community

that was posturing itself for transterritorial witness to all people, including Jews in Palestine.

5. Warfare remained a viable option in Jesus' day, as evident in the guerilla tactics of the zealots. Yet Jesus remained faithful to the Jeremianic alternative. He continued the formation of God's people as a peaceful witness to the nations. The Holy Spirit furthered that formation after Pentecost by scattering God's people across the globe to mediate God's peace to all nations.

This revision transcends marcionite dualism and strengthens the continuity position by establishing a strong connection not only between the God of the conquest and the cross but also between diaspora Israel and the scattered church. Moreover, it is dynamic enough to encompass the best insights of plurality approaches. The Israelites were neither consistent pacifists nor just war theorists. Indeed their diverse sociological configurations required that they relate to opposition in diverse ways. This need not mean, however, that the Israelites operated under constantly fluctuating and competing ethical frameworks. If Yoder's revision is right, God had always required the Israelites to rely on him alone for their well-being, and he did this precisely so he may later scatter them throughout the world as his peaceful witnesses. The consistency of this narrative is not negated by the fact that the Israelites were neither fully aware of God's plan nor completely faithful in executing it. Indeed, another consistent trajectory in Israel and the church's story is that God's people seldom follow God's instructions perfectly and that God often uses their detours to accomplish his purposes. So we need not choose between plurality and continuity. When it comes to warfare in Scripture, there is plurality in the context of movement in a consistent direction. Whatever deviates from this trajectory may be regarded as unfaithful on grounds internal to *both* testaments.

Thus the "problem" of biblical warfare is not Scripture's alleged inconsistency from one testament to the other. It is the reader's failure to discern in Scripture how, from the very beginning, God identified bloodshed as a problem and has been shaping his people ever since to resist its deadly allure. The turning point in this shaping was the Diaspora of Jeremiah; its culmination was the gospel of Jesus Christ.

Notes

1. Judith E. Sanderson offers an extremely helpful though somewhat dated survey of the field in "War, Peace, and Justice in the Hebrew Bible: A Representative Bibliography," in the English translation of Gerhard von Rad's *Holy War in Ancient Israel*, (Grand Rapids, MI: Eerdmans, 1991), 135-66.

2. Although I am engaging only the past four decades of scholarship, the early church employed similar techniques for dealing with this question. Cf. Roland H. Bainton, *Christian Attitudes Toward War and Peace: A Historical Survey and Critical Evaluation* (Nashville: Abingdon Press, 1960), 82.

3. E.g., Cyril Rodd, *Glimpses of a Strange Land*, Studies in Old Testament Ethics (Edinburgh: T & T Clark, 2001), 185-206; and Willard M. Swartley, *Slavery, Sabbath, War and Women* (Scottdale, PA: Herald Press, 1983).

4. E.g., Susan Niditch, *War in the Hebrew Bible: A Study in the Ethics of Violence* (New York: Oxford, 1993); Lynn Jost, "Warfare in the Old Testament: An Argument for Peacemaking in the New Millennium," *Direction* 27, no. 2 (1998): 177-88; Paul D. Hanson, "War and Peace in the Hebrew Bible," *Interpretation* 38, no. 4 (1984): 341-62; T. R. Hobbs, *A Time for War: A Study of Warfare in the Old Testament*, Old Testament Studies 4 (Wilmington, DE: Michael Glazier, 1989); and Michael Walzer, "The Idea of Holy War in Ancient Israel," *Journal of Religious Ethics* 20, no. 2 (1992): 215-28.

5. E.g., Lois Barrett, *The Way God Fights: War and Peace in the Old Testament* (Scottdale, PA: Herald Press, 1987); Peter C. Craigie, *The Problem of War in the Old Testament* (Grand Rapids, MI: Eerdmans, 1978); Gary Hall, "Violence in the Name of God: Israel's Holy Wars," in *Christian Ethics: The Issues of Life and Death*, ed. Larry Chouinard, et al, 261-84 (Joplin, MO: Parma Press, 2003); Waldemar Janzen, "God as Warrior and Lord: A Conversation with G. E. Wright," *Bulletin of the American Schools of Oriental Research*, no. 220 (1975): 73-75; Jeph Holloway, "The Ethical Dilemma of Holy War," *Southwestern Journal of Theology* 41, no. 1 (1998): 44-69; and John A. Wood, *Perspectives on War in the Bible* (Macon, GA: Mercer University, 1998).

6. I chose the term "biblical warfare" over "Old Testament warfare" to establish some much needed space between warfare and the Old Testament. If Yoder is right, warfare is not an "Old Testament practice" but a web of practices that tempted God's people in both testaments.

7. John Howard Yoder, "If Abraham is Our Father" in *The Original Revolution; Essays on Christian Pacifism* (Scottdale, PA: Herald Press, 1971), 91-111.

8. At this time Yoder was especially dependent upon Millard Lind's unpublished dissertation "The Theology of Warfare in Ancient Israel," Western Theological Seminary (1963); and von Rad's *Der Heilige Krieg im Alten Israel* (Göttingen: Vandenhoeck and Ruprecht, 1952).

9. "God Will Fight for Us," in John Howard Yoder, *The Politics of Jesus*, 2nd ed. (Grand Rapids, MI: Eerdmans, 1994), 76-88. It may be worth noting that Yoder points out in this essay that when Israel took warfare into its own hands, the results were often disastrous. This serves as a commentary on what happens when Israel abandons the holy war posture.

10. Much of this work has been gathered and published after Yoder's untimely death in 1997 as *The Jewish-Christian Schism Revisited* (Grand Rapids, MI: Eerdmans, 2003)—a work that Yoder himself was planning to complete and submit for publication.

11. It should be noted that the direction Yoder heads in these essays is already anticipated in his essays engaging liberation theology. See "Exodus: Probing the Meaning of Liberation," *Sojourners*, September 1976, 26-29; and "Exodus and Exile: The Two Faces of Liberation," *Cross Currents* 23, no. 3 (1973): 297-309.

12. Millard Lind, *Yahweh is a Warrior* (Scottdale: Herald Press, 1980). Yoder makes a passing reference to this concept in a lecture delivered the year before but not published until much later, entitled: "The Bible and Civil Turmoil," in *For the Nations: Essays Public and Evangelical* (Grand Rapids, MI: Eerdmans, 1997), 86; and "Exodus 20:13—'Thou Shalt Not Kill,'" *Interpretation* 34, no. 4 (1980): 398.

13. Yoder, "Introduction," in Lind *Yahweh is a Warrior*, 18.

14. John Howard Yoder, "Jesus the Jewish Pacifist," 70-71. This essay was originally delivered as a Bethel College lecture in 1982 and was later published in *The Jewish-Christian Schism Revisited*, 69-89.

15. John Howard Yoder, "To Your Tents, O Israel," 35, in *Studies in Religion/Sciences Religieuses* 18, no. 3 (1989): 345-62.

16. John Howard Yoder, "Texts that Summon or Texts that Serve: A Response to Michael Walzer," *Journal of Religious Ethics* 20, no. 2 (1992): 229-34. Michael Walzer, "The Idea of Holy War in Ancient Israel," *Journal of Religious Ethics* 20, no. 2 (1992): 215-28.

17. John Howard Yoder, "See How They Go with Their Face to the Sun," in *Jewish-Christian Schism Revisited*, 186.

18. Yoder, "See How They Go with Their Face to the Sun," 187.

19. E.g., Abraham's many attempts to engineer the fulfillment of God's promise of offspring, like bringing Lot along with him (against God's command) and impregnating Sarah's maidservant, Hagar.

20. These warnings seem to be based on Deut 17:14-20 where Moses tells the Israelites that they will later set up a king and warns against how such a king should and should not reign. The kingship fell well short of Moses' vision.

21. Walter Brueggemann underscores this point in *Prophetic Imagination* (Philadelphia: Fortress Press, 1978), 21-38.

22. For a while it appeared that Zerubbabel may assume the throne (Hag 2:20-23), but he mysteriously drops off the scene and is never mentioned again. So despite their grand expectations for full national restoration, the dust settled and the people could only mourn the insignificance of their half-restored status (Ezra 3:8-13; Hag 2:1-3). Ezra himself narrates Israel's postexilic existence as continued enslavement (Neh 9:36).

23. Dan 11:34 may allude to the Maccabeans as "a little help"— but aside from such faint praise, there is nothing. The force of this point would be diluted, however, if it could be demonstrated that Daniel was written prior to the Maccabean revolt. A robust reading of the book of Daniel would contribute significantly to Yoder's argument, yet he makes surprisingly little use of it.

24. This was the case during the time of the patriarchs (ca. 1900-1700 BC), Egyptian enslavement (ca. 1700-1300 BC), wilderness wanderings (ca. 1300-1250 BC), Exile and Babylonian occupation (ca. 587-539 BC), Persian occupation (ca. 539-333 BC), Greek occupation (ca. 333-168 BC), and eventually under Rome. Israel only briefly existed in the land without foreign oversight (ca. 1250-587 BC), but these years were far from glorious. They were typified by domestic violence, internal collusion, border skirmishes, illicit alliances, excessive warfare, and overall failure to trust God alone. The biblical historians make little effort to cover this up.

25. A. James Reimer, "Mennonites, Christ, and Culture: The Yoder Legacy," *Conrad Grebel Review* 16, no. 2 (1998): 8-9.

26. Peter Ochs, in *The Jewish-Christian Schism Revisited*, 204. In this piece, Ochs briefly responds to each of Yoder's essays.

27. John Goldingay, *Old Testament Theology: Israel's Gospel* (Downers Grove, IL: InterVarsity, 2003), 764.

28. Paul J. Kissling, "Can John Howard Yoder's Ethics Embrace the

Entire Old Testament as Scripture?" A paper presented at the November 17, 2005, gathering of Evangelical Theological Society in Valley Forge, PA.

29. See Jer 3:14-17; 33:4-18.

30. E.g., Isa 60:1-22; Zech 14:3-21.

31. E.g., Baruch and 1 Esdras are affirming; 1 Enoch is not (e.g., 72:13; 83-90, 92-105). What is remarkable about 1 Enoch is how its various books retell the events of Israel's life from its beginning until the second century and entirely omit the sixth-century return from exile and refortification.

32. Yoder spells out his biblical realist approach to Scripture in various essays collected in *To Hear the Word* (Eugene, OR: Wipf and Stock, 2001).

33. In "See How They Go," for instance, Yoder refers to Ezra and Nehemiah as "politicking elders" and negatively narrates their work as "too early returns to the land," "inappropriate deviations from the Jeremiah line," and a "mistake," 193-94. It is interesting to note, however, that scholars do not critique Yoder's equally negative narration of the monarchy. This is partly because of the strong anti-monarchical strands in Scripture itself and partly because this critique has a longer history in biblical scholarship, e.g., Brueggemann's *Prophetic Imagination*.

34. See David J. A. Clines, *The Theme of the Pentateuch* (Sheffield: JSOT Press, 1997).

35. In *Ezekiel and the Ethics of Exile* (New York: Oxford University Press, 2001), Andrew Mein—who shows no evidence of having read Yoder—argues persuasively that Ezekiel begins reshaping Israel's ethical framework in ways quite similar to Yoder. He concludes that there is a shift from civil responsibility to passivity, by which he means that Israel's restoration would not be a response to human effort or even repentance but God's sole initiative (255). In his words, "Decisions and actions which might realistically bring about a national restoration no longer form part of their moral world. The passivity of the people mirrors their social and political impotence as exiles" (256). His reading of Ezra and Nehemiah also compliments Yoder's project. For instance, he narrates Ezra's intermarriage condemnation in terms of survival of a minority witness on hostile soil (161) and Nehemiah's call for divorce as a means of squelching political alliances that would also threaten that witness (160).

36. Although one could argue that the apostle Paul sought to visit Jerusalem at that time as a gesture of solidarity toward Jews who would

gather there.

37. Though this sending forth from Jerusalem may be used to support palestinocentrism, one could also argue that God sought to get Israel back on track with his transterritorial purposes precisely at the point where Israel went off track, thereby meeting them once again at their point of offense.

38. Beyond this, it should be noted, there is little emphasis on Jerusalem in the New Testament. If anything, we see the opposite. This begins with Jesus' words to the Samaritan woman that the day had come during which true worship is not restricted to Jerusalem (John 4:20-24). It continues with Paul's allegory identifying the Jerusalem of his time with slavery and the "Jerusalem above" with freedom (Gal 4:25-26). Finally, in contrast to Ezekiel, the seer of the Apocalypse envisions a future time—not when the old Jerusalem is restored—but when a "New Jerusalem" descends from heaven (Rev 3:12; 21:2, 10). Though this could be a symbolic way of depicting a restored Jerusalem, the descent from heaven at least indicates that God will have to be the source of this restoration, not ecclesial engineering (like the stone not cut out by human hands in Dan 2:24).

39. This should not surprise us since God often fulfilled his promises to Israel in ways that differed from Israel's expressed expectations in Scripture. The nature of the return from exile is one example. The advent of the Messiah in two installments is another.

40. See James 1:1; 1 Pet 1:1, 17; 2:11; Phil 3:20.

41. In *Jesus, the Tribulation, and the End of the Exile: Restoration Eschatology and the Origin of the Atonement* (Grand Rapids, MI: Baker, 2005), Brant Pitre persuasively argues that it muddles matters to think of the return from exile as another form of exiled existence. The quality of life may be similar, he argues, but the term "exile" is emptied of its meaning if applied to life in one's homeland. Less convincingly, Pitre goes on to argue that language of the "end of exile" is also misleading because so few Jews actually returned and there is no mention of the return of those exiles who were originally scattered from the northern kingdom. For Pitre, the exile does not end until the northern exiles are reunited to both the southern exiles and those who never moved, which ultimately takes place in Christ's atoning work.

42. Similarly, the short-lived Maccabean project dispelled all myths that humanly engineered independence might usher in the kingdom.

43. I am not claiming that bloodshed is the only sin or even the pri-

mary sin. I am simply noting God's stance toward this particular sin from its inception.

Contributors

Andy Alexis-Baker graduated from Associated Mennonite Biblical Seminary in Elkhart, Indiana, and has been an Adjunct Professor of Peace, Justice and Conflict Studies at Goshen (Indiana) College. He has published two articles in the *Conrad Grebel Review* on Mennonites and policing, and a book chapter in *Electing Not to Vote*, edited by Ted Lewis. He is the co-editor, with Ted Koontz, of John Howard Yoder's *Christian Attitudes to War, Peace, and Revolution* (Brazos Press, 2009). He is currently working on a manuscript on Christianity and policing.

Nekeisha Alexis-Baker received her Masters of Arts: Theological Studies degree from Associated Mennonite Biblical Seminary with a concentration in theology and ethics. She received her Bachelor of Arts degree from New York University, where she majored in Africana Studies. Currently, her research interests include animal ethics and creation care from a Christian perspective, and the intersection between anarchist politics and Christian faith. She is also actively engaged in anti-racist activism and authored the essay "Freedom of Voice: Non-Voting and the Political Imagination" in *Electing Not to Vote*.

Jeremy M. Bergen is Assistant Professor of Religious Studies and Theology at Conrad Grebel University College, University of Waterloo. His PhD dissertation at the University of St. Michael's College (Toronto School of Theology) was a theological analysis of the practice of ecclesial repentance and the nature the church. He has published articles on topics such as martyrdom, Mennonite–Catholic dialogue, reconciliation, and biblical interpretation. With Paul G. Doerksen and Karl Koop, he is the co-editor of *Creed and Conscience: Essays in Honour of A. James Reimer* (Pandora Press, 2007).

Richard Bourne is Senior Lecturer in Theology and Ethics at the University of Cumbria in the United Kingdom. He previously held teaching positions at Trinity and All Saints College, Leeds, and the Open Theological College (University of Gloucestershire). He received his PhD in Theology from the University of Exeter in 2005. Bourne is the author of *Seek the Peace of the City: Christian Political Criticism as Public, Realist and Transformative* (Cascade, forthcoming).

Andrew Brubacher Kaethler teaches youth ministry and directs !Explore: A Theological Program for High School Youth at Associated Mennonite Biblical Seminary. He is completing his PhD at Garrett-Evangelical Theological Seminary in Evanston, Illinois, focusing on theological and philosophical considerations regarding identity in the shift from modernity to postmodernity. His research interests also include the philosophy of technology and philosophy of science. He is an ordained minister who has served in ministry positions in Mennonite Church Eastern Canada.

Paul C. Heidebrecht is a Lecturer in the Department of Theology at Marquette University, where he received his PhD in Religious Studies in 2008. He is also a graduate of the University of Waterloo and Associated Mennonite Biblical Seminary, and has worked for several years as a mechanical engineer in the automotive industry.

Chris K. Huebner is Associate Professor of Theology and Philosophy at Canadian Mennonite University. His work focuses on questions that might be located at the intersection of knowledge and politics. He is the author of *A Precarious Peace: Yoderian Explorations on Theology, Knowledge, and Identity* (Herald Press, 2006) and is currently working on a book about martyrdom, knowledge, and the theological virtues.

Paul Martens is an Assistant Professor of Religion at Baylor University. He received his PhD (Theology, 2005) from the University of Notre Dame, and his research is focused on the relationship between religion and morality. He has published numerous articles concerning the theological ethics of John Howard Yoder, the thought of Søren Kierkegaard, and other themes in Christian ethics.

John C. Nugent is Professor of Old Testament at Great Lakes Christian College in Lansing, Michigan. His PhD is from Calvin Theological Seminary where he wrote a dissertation on Yoder's appropriation of the Old Testament for ecclesiology. He holds additional graduate degrees from Duke Divinity School (ThM) and Emmanuel School of Religion (MDiv). Nugent has published articles in academic and popular level journals and is currently editing a collection of essays on Yoder for ACU Press titled *Radical Ecumenicity.*

Branson Parler is Assistant Professor of Theology at Kuyper College in Grand Rapids, Michigan. He is a PhD candidate at Calvin Theological Seminary, where he is writing his dissertation on the interrelation of Christ, creation, and culture in Yoder. He has presented conference papers on figures such as Augustine and Abraham Kuyper. His research interests include christology, ecclesiology, and theological accounts of culture.

Anthony G. Siegrist is Assistant Professor of Bible and Theology at Prairie College in Three Hills, Alberta. He holds an MA from Eastern Mennonite Seminary and is a ThD candidate in systematic theology at Wycliffe College, Toronto School of Theology. Siegrist has written and done editorial work at both the scholarly and popular level. He is currently writing his dissertation on believers baptism.

Philip E. Stoltzfus is Visiting Professor of Justice and Peace Studies at the University of St. Thomas, in St. Paul, Minnesota. He holds MDiv and ThD degrees from Harvard Divinity School. He previously taught in the religion departments at Bethel College, North Newton, Kansas, and St. Olaf College, Northfield, Minnesota. He is author of *Theology as Performance: Music, Aesthetics, and God in Western Thought* (T. & T. Clark, 2006). His areas of interest include modern constructive theology, theological aesthetics, and liberation theologies.